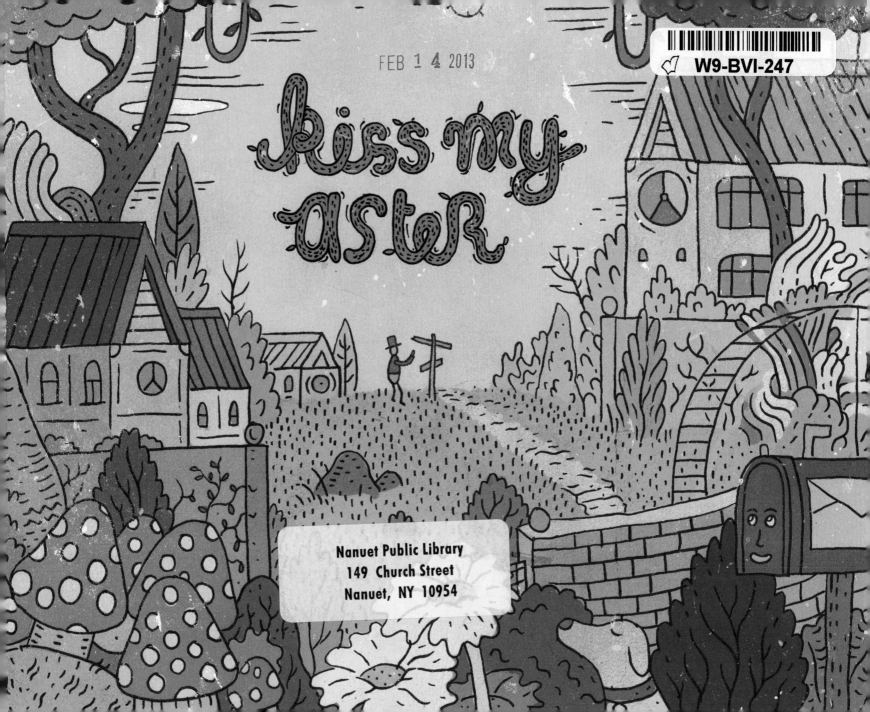

kiss my aster

KISS my

A Graphic Guide to Creating a Fantastic Yard Totally Tailored to You

Aster

Amanda Thomsen

Illustrations by Am I Collective

Storey Publishing

The mission of Storey Publishing is to serve our customers by publishing practical information that encourages personal independence in harmony with the environment.

Edited by Carleen Madigan
Art direction by Carolyn Eckert
Book design by Am I Collective
Text production by Liseann Karandisecky and Jennifer Jepson Smith

Illustrations © Am I Collective/ Bernstein & Andriulli
Author's photograph by © Julie Fehler

Storey books are available for special premium and promotional uses and for customized editions.

For further information, please call 1-800-793-9396.

Storey Publishing
210 MASS MoCA Way
North Adams, MA 01247
www.storey.com

Printed in China by R.R. Donnelley
10 9 8 7 6 5 4 3 2 1

Library of Congress Cataloging-in-Publication Data

Thomsen, Amanda.
  Kiss my aster / by Amanda Thomsen.
    p. cm.
  Includes index.
  ISBN 978-1-60342-986-3 (pbk. ~ alk. paper)
  1. Landscape gardening. 2. Landscape design. I. Title.
SB473.T5525 2013
635.9~dc23

To **Dan**, for babysitting and more

To **Bob**, for everything

To my **parents**, for not asking how the book was going (out of fear)

To **Carleen**, for finding me in a dumpster and making me an author

To **Hazel**, may you never have white lava rock in your front yard

Introduction

I was thinking: Books today aren't very interactive, in a world that's increasingly interactive. If something doesn't beep, flash, or tweet at me, I hardly know it exists. Then I started to daydream about what I could do to make a book that was more engaging. Perhaps there could be a tiny robot on each page, or maybe I could include a kitten with each copy. Then I remembered the Choose Your Own Adventure books I read by the score in the 1980s, and I realized that this series, along with anything that invites you to write, color, lick, sniff, or scratch in it, is just about as interactive as it gets. So the question was: Could I make a book about gardening and landscaping in that style?

Here, you're not deciding whether to enter the haunted cave or to use that time machine. Or where

to hide the body (well, actually, I think I address that on page 71). You're deciding whether you should plant that tree or hire someone to do it for you, and if you have what it takes to grow your own vegetables ~ or should you just stick with the farmers' market? Should you put in irrigation or water your yard using a setup of straws and duct tape? What kind of garden would grow in a haunted cave, anyway?

The bonus? You don't have to read the whole book ~ just the stuff that pertains to you and what you think you want to do in your outdoor space. At the bottom of each page you decide where to go next, so there's never any overkill. This way, the book is rather interactive and totally tailored to you.

Also? It's pretty funny.

Things you might want to know about . . .

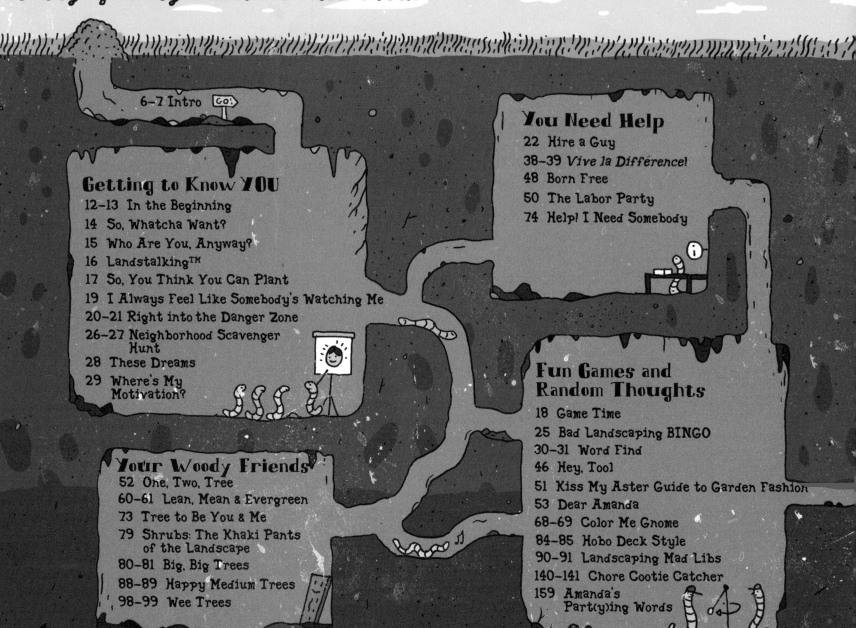

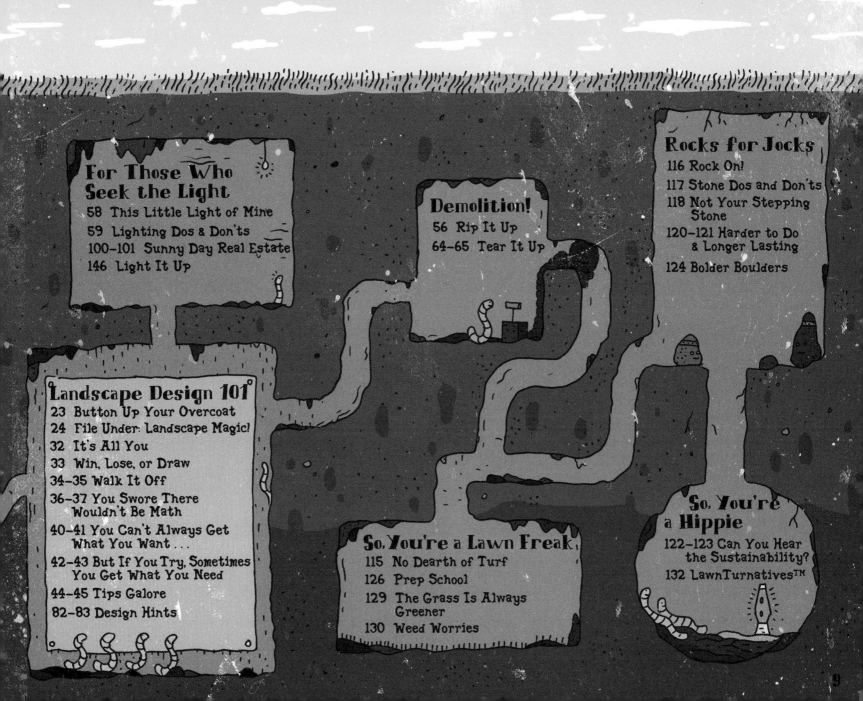

In The Beginning...

Does the area around your house have that not-so-fresh feeling? Did you move into a house with 20 years of someone else's bum landscaping? Does your yard have all the appeal of a cheap hotel bedspread? Or do you have a brand, spankin'-new house with lame, builder-installed "foundation plantings"? Maybe you just want your outside space to look a little different from that of the Joneses. And who can blame you? The Joneses are bore-ring. They're a little bit country and you're

You don't have to have the greatest yard in the world; it just has to be nicer than your worst neighbor's.

You can keep your enemies out of your house, but they can drive by anytime and make fun of you.

a little bit rock 'n' roll. This book will help you trick out your yard in 375 (or fewer) simple and/or back-breaking steps, and every step will be all about you.

Your landscaping is just as much an expression of your style as your rugs, curtains, or Hello Kitty waffle iron are. Curb appeal is as important as your dining room chairs. Frighteningly, your yard is exposed to the world and leaves an impression on everyone who passes by, revealing who you are and what you think is cool.

Turn to So, Whatcha Want? (Page 14), to figure out what exactly you're getting yourself into.

So, WHATCHA WANT?

So, what do you really want and what are you really willing to do to get it? Are you looking to rip out the existing landscaping and put in new beds full of plants you love? Do you want a new deck or patio? A paddock for your unicorns? A place to party? A place for the rug rats to play? A place for Fido to poop? Could you use some shade? Want to swap that resource-intensive lawn for something more earth-friendly? Do you want a wee bit more curb appeal?

Are you trying to sell your house? Do you need privacy from your neighbors? Do you need a paddock for your prizewinning skunks? Do you want a patio to party on, so you can wiggle it, just a little bit? How about a zipline that goes from your roof to your hot tub? Yeah, that's not gonna happen.

At this point, don't let money hinder you. **Dream big, baby, and get out the crayons.**

Turn to Landstalking™ (page 16) to learn how to be a landscape spy.

To learn what will thrive in your climate and what will croak, turn to Right into the Danger Zone (page 20).

Overwhelmed? Don't be you're just reading a book! Wait until you're knee-deep in quick-set concrete before you freak out.

Who Are You, Anyway?

What kind of gardener do you think you are?

When you go into a garden store you:

A Head for the gravel samples and shrub selections
B Run to the vegetable seeds
C Look at all the pretty flowers
D You don't even know where there is a garden center and if you did, you'd never actually go inside

What do you like about your landscaping?

A Nothing. That's why you're reading this book.
B It's okay. You just wish you had some homegrown tomatoes to slice and put on top of it.
C It's okay, but it lacks pretty flowers
D You call this landscaping?

When you go on vacation:

A You notice different places have different styles of landscaping
B You notice different places have local foods, available seasonally
C Look at all the pretty flowers!
D You're sleeping the whole time, so you notice nothing

Your wardrobe is:

A Utilitarian
B Made from organic materials, and sustainable like crazy
C All floral prints
D What kind of stupid question is that?

How do you feel about hardware stores?

A Everybody knows you in yours.
B You found one that is local (not a big box) and woman-owned
C Um . . .
D You hire people to do that for you

MOSTLY A:
YOU ARE A WEEKEND WARRIOR, UP TO THE CHALLENGE OF RIPPING OUT YOUR FRONT YARD AND REPLACING IT WITH A WONDERLAND OF SHRUBBERY.

MOSTLY B:
YOU WERE BORN TO BE A FARMER, BUT YOU MOST LIKELY DON'T LIVE ON A FARM. YOU NEED TO GROW YOUR OWN, AND BY THAT I MEAN FOOD.

MOSTLY C:
FLOWER POWER! YOU WANT TO SPICE UP YOUR 'SCAPE WITH ALL THINGS PRETTY AND PETALED! THEN HAVE A TEA PARTY!

MOSTLY D:
YOU WANT TO GET A FEW CHUCKLES FROM THIS BOOK, THEN HIRE SOMEONE TO DO EVERYTHING. AND THAT'S OKAY.

Land-stalking™

The easiest way to figure out where to start your outdoor transformation is to walk around the neighborhood (or drive yourself to a trendier, feistier, more classic, or more modern neighborhood — whatever is going to inspire you) and really look at what your neighbors are growing.

I call this Landstalking™. If something is growing well for your neighbors, it's going to do all right for you. Not that I'm condoning the cookie-cutter school of design. I would never! But it's nice to have a pile of "knowns" and "unknowns" in life — even if it's just in your landscape.

HOME LANDSCAPING IS JUST LIKE A MULLET: business in front and party in back. You can't go wrong with a simple, structured front yard.

What looks COOL?

What's in the FRONT YARD?

What are the walks & drives made out of?

What's the ratio of lawn to flowerbeds?

What's in between the HOUSES for PRIVACY?

What's overused? What looks AWFUL?

Are there people out there using THE SPACE?

How do the neighbors express their INDIVIDUALITY?

What plants look good to you?

DECISION: Get the most out of your Landstalking™ by turning to I Always Feel Like Somebody's Watching Me (page 19). If you think you're ready to roll, try It's All You (page 32).

So, you think you can plant

Wait ~

I didn't mention that you should start buying plants yet~ unless you really think you're the shiznit. Because you know nothing of planting, yo. **Nothing.**

1. Have you called for someone to do a locate for cable TV lines, electric cables, and gas lines? Every state has a hotline to call before you dig: Someone comes to your house to mark where, you know, all the underground lines are. Can you see the value to this? I hope so. It's the law, and it's free. To find your local number, on the Web, search for your state and "underground locate."

2. One thing you need to figure out, quickly, is what it's going to cost you. Price out the different ideas for your yard, area by area, with the plant recommendations and info you got at the garden center. What I do is write each price, in red, on the space it would occupy on the plan. Then I decide which areas are affordable and doable in, say, a weekend. We do like immediate gratification, don't we . . .

3. It's amazing how an area that's affordable and doable in one weekend is also about as much, physically, as one normal, out-of-shape person can do. Funny how that works out.

4. Do you have all the necessary tools? The shovels, the wheelbarrows? The buzzwazzles? The splinkblinkers?

Time to do this thing. Flip on over to Hey, TOOL (page 46) to figure out what you'll need.

Not interested in getting physical? **Hire a Guy** (page 22) may be just what the doctor ordered.

You and your outdoor space are getting serious. Are you ready to go steady?

Let's talk design principles.

The very first thing you should know about is appropriateness. The style of your home lends itself to a certain kind of landscaping. For example, an old farmhouse would probably look silly with a formal boxwood parterre in the front yard. A Georgian home would be absurd with a modern gravel-and-bamboo look. That said, just because all your neighbors have a certain style doesn't mean it's the correct one for their architecture (or for yours), so your Landstalking™ adventures (page 16) may not clue you in to this. It's likely they just have what's easiest.

HOUSE STYLE	GARDEN
1. High-rise condo	**A.** Eclectic perennial garden
2. Arts and Crafts bungalow	**B.** Formal boxwood hedges
3. Greek Revival	**C.** Simple trees with little ornamentation
4. Farmhouse	**D.** Casual plantings or native insect sanctuary
5. Modern	**E.** Bamboo, grasses, lots of hardscape
6. Victorian manor	**F.** Native plants with encroaching invasives, empty bean cans
7. Santa's house	**G.** Bonsai cherry trees
8. Munchkin manor	**H.** Window boxes and indoor plants that get rolled out to the balcony for summer
9. Abandoned freight car	**I.** Giant, sparkly candy canes

Sometimes a bland house just begs for a bland landscape. I hope you don't find yourself in this situation.

Answer Key: Farmhouse=Eclectic perennial garden; Modern=Bamboo, grasses, lots of hardscape; Greek Revival=Simple trees with little ornamentation; Victorian manor=Formal boxwood hedges; Arts and Crafts bungalow=Casual plantings or native insect sanctuary; High-rise condo=Window boxes and indoor plants; Santa's house=Giant, sparkly candy canes; Munchkin manor=Bonsai cherry trees

I ALWAYS FEEL LIKE SOMEBODY'S WATCHING ME

So you're going on an idea hunt around your 'hood (or someone else's). Why not bring a digital camera and snap some pics? Make sure you're respectful of people's privacy, though; take your photos from the sidewalk or even farther away. Your goal is better landscaping, not a restraining order. An air of nonchalance and a phone with a camera are perfect for this task. Taking photos of the neighbors' yards is a great way to find out which plants do well in your climate.

Props to help the Landstalking™ go more smoothly:

A baby carriage (with or without a baby in it) or a dog (yours or borrowed). This way you can pretend to be snapping photos of your baby and/or dog but really be snapping away at gorgeous landscapes.

Did you even think that you'd be getting exercise while all this Landstalking™ is going on? I wouldn't wear a leg warmers/head band/ wrist bands combination, though. They may raise suspicion...

Make sure to bring the whole family on these neighborhood romps. You don't want a yard that only reflects your needs and taste, do you? Oh, I see...You do...

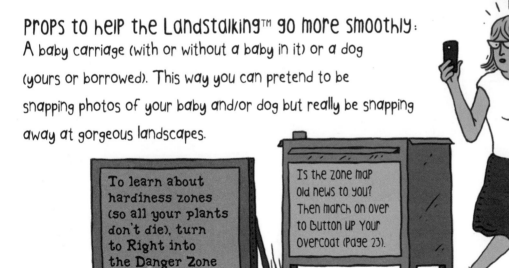

To learn about hardiness zones (so all your plants don't die), turn to Right into the Danger Zone (page 20).

Is the zone map old news to you? Then march on over to Button Up Your Overcoat (page 23).

Right into the Danger Zone

What's all this zone business, anyway?

You have a zone; you must learn to use it. Your zone tells you the average coldest winter temperature in your area, and with that information, you can grow perennials that will actually come back in the spring. There's an official USDA Zone Hardiness Map, but the one on the facing page is funnier. Use this map, or the boring USDA one, to figure out what zone you're in.

Then you can determine which zones your friends are in and call them in the middle of the night to let them know. So, if you're living in Zone 5 and you find a plant that's labeled as hardy in Zones 2~4, you know you're dealing with the Mr. T of plants. Or if you're in Zone 8 and you like a plant that's hardy in Zones 4~6, you're gonna fry that plant in no time. Got it?

It's good to know about zone hardiness if you're shopping at a big-box store; you can't rely on it to stock only hardy plants. It's also awesome for buying plants on the Internet, which I highly recommend. Bring a cocktail, and pants are optional.

> To learn more about what to do with the photos of your neighbors (I mean neighbors' properties), check out File Under: Landscape Magic! (page 24).
>
> If you'd prefer to skip to the meat and potatoes, try It's All You (page 32).

> Zone envy is natural, but each of us has good things that no one else can have. And I wouldn't have it any other way.

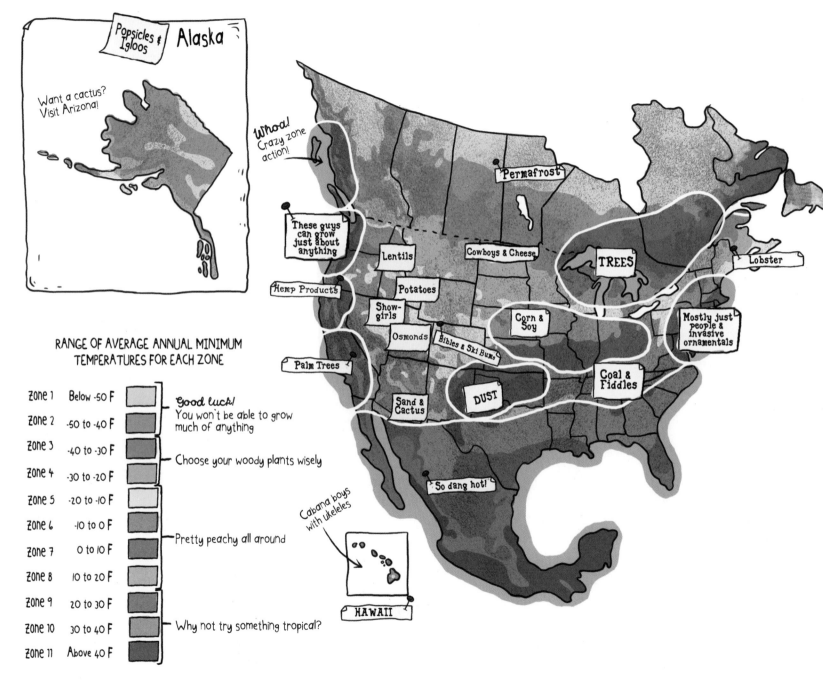

Popsicles &
Igloos   Alaska

Want a cactus?
Visit Arizona!

Whoa!
Crazy zone
action!

Permafrost

These guys
can grow
just about
anything

Lentils   Cowboys & Cheese   TREES   Lobster

Hemp Products   Potatoes

Show-
girls   Corn &   Mostly just
         Osmonds   Bibles & Ski Bums   Soy   people &
                                                         invasive
                                                         ornamentals

Palm Trees   Coal &
                                               Fiddles

RANGE OF AVERAGE ANNUAL MINIMUM
TEMPERATURES FOR EACH ZONE   Sand &   DUST
                                    Cactus

Zone 1   Below -50 F   Good luck!
                           You won't be able to grow
Zone 2   -50 to -40 F   much of anything

Zone 3   -40 to -30 F   Choose your woody plants wisely

Zone 4   -30 to -20 F
                                              So dang hot!
Zone 5   -20 to -10 F

Zone 6   -10 to 0 F   Cabana boys
                           with ukeleles
                           Pretty peachy all around
Zone 7   0 to 10 F

Zone 8   10 to 20 F

Zone 9   20 to 30 F

Zone 10   30 to 40 F   Why not try something tropical?

Zone 11   Above 40 F   HAWAII

21

Hire a guy

There's no shame in this game.
I applaud you for knowing that you're in over your head, and I think it's huge that you're going to read ahead because you want to know enough to make informed decisions. Whether you want out entirely or just need someone to put the icing on your landscake, it's best to understand how things work. You want to know just enough to be dangerous, right?

In landscaping, there's no right or wrong. If you feel like you can't handle doing it yourself . . . you're doing it right.

To figure out the difference between a **landscape architect** and a **garden designer**, flip to *Vive la Différence!* (page 38).

If you have the total package and want someone to mow and maintain it, flip to The Labor Party (Page 50).

If you want to be **your own designer** but to hire someone else to install it, flip to It's All You (page 32).

Get out your checkbook.

Button Up Your Overcoat

I recommend doing neighborhood walk-throughs over a period of months to get a clear picture of what's going on. Landscapes change almost daily, if you can believe it. Some evergreens are hardly noticeable in July but shout "HOLD THE GUACAMOLE!" in December. In springtime, everything is glorious, but if you only plan for spring blooms, the rest of your calendar will be about as exciting

Planning and research can be done via the Internet, with the help of garden center gurus, or by paying someone to do all the fancy figurin' for you.

Turn to File Under: Landscape Magic! (page 24) to get this train a-rollin'.

Or how about a little game to help figure out which landscape style is most appropriate for your crib? Turn to Game Time, page 18.

as smooth jazz. You want to make sure that no matter what time of year you look out your window or pull into your driveway, there's something you love to see. This is accomplished with planning and research. Are you up for that? There's no final exam, and no unpleasant side effects.

JUST SO YOU KNOW, perennials are plants that come back every year, but they usually don't bloom all summer. Most flower for less than a month. Annuals bloom all summer long but need to be replaced every year.

If you buy all your plants at one time and they're all in bloom, you've screwed up. Chances are that they'll bloom for only a few weeks, then deflate on the anniversary of your purchase.

LANDSCAPE MAGIC!

'SPY STUFF'

Have you taken a ton of photos of random people's landscapes? Well, now it's time to print them up and keep them in a special folder labeled LANDSCAPING (or, if that's too predictable, SPY STUFF). Next, take these mystery plant photos to a garden center to have them identified. Write down everything the people helping you say about the plants and keep the notes in your LANDSCAPING (or SPY STUFF) file. Make sure to ask about maximum size, growth rate, if it flowers or fruits, if birds love it, if reindeer love it, if it has cool bark or beautiful fall color, if it knows any good ghost stories, and if it has special requirements. Most important, ask if it does well in your area. And for bonus points, ask the folks you corner if they would use it in their own yard.

That's the real deal, right there.

EXPERTS:

Keep in mind that not everyone in a garden center is an expert: Some are experts on one subject, some are know-it-alls, and some are really good at loading bags of soil into your trunk. Put on your best sad face and whine "I need BIG help" when you go through the door, and pray to be directed to the right person.

seeds

GARDEN CENTERS:

Don't go to the garden center for this much help on a Saturday morning or during any other peak time. Or five minutes before closing. You want a calm, relaxed, knowledgeable person to help you without the pressure of other shoppers waiting with their own questions. So go on a lazy weekday afternoon. And don't bring more than a few photos at a time.

HEY! DO NOT STEAL INFO TAGS from the pots in a garden center, it brings really bad JUJU. Nowadays some tags have QR codes you can scan, so use those, yo.

Garden shoes!

DAD...

DELICIOUS monster

Aren't you glad that's done? You deserve a round of Bad Landscaping Bingo (page 25). Ready to design your own landscape? Turn to It's All You, page 32.

BAD LANDSCAPING

BINGO

B	I	N	G	O
White rock mulch	Lawn damaged by dog pee	Dyed red mulch	Planter made from an old tire	Big tree too close to the house
Lawn is more than 25% weeds	Giant boulder in front yard for no reason	More cement than living stuff	No privacy from the nosy neighbors	Military-style pruning
Vines are taking over	Deer have eaten everything down to the nubs	FREE	Boxes piled up in the front yard like it's a foreclosure	Giant plastic playset in clear view
Oops you forgot to water. Welcome to the Dead Zone	Gas grill that's bigger than your car	Gnomes	More than two topiaries*	More than one item of statuary
Statue of little boy peeing	Tree faces	The "I'll take one of everything" look	Fake deer	an old Chevy up on blocks
Too much mulch	An old toilet	A topped tree	Empty pots	Weeds that are taller than you are

*Unless your name is Pearl Fryar

~ Neighborhood ~
SCAVENGER HUNT

When you're reconnoitering and searching for ideas and inspiration, think of it as a scavenger hunt (extra points if you wear a superhero costume). Be on the lookout for:

Evergreens. See if you can find gigantic spruce and teensy-weensy boxwood, and everything in between. There are some very un-boring evergreens out there, and if you live in a cool climate, they make the skeleton of your landscaping in winter. ☐

Shrubs. There's no easier, faster way to change the look of your space than to tear out some mangy old shrubs and replace them with cool ones. And there are cool ones. (See page 79.) ☐

Tall trees/street trees. Maybe you're out of your league considering an 80-foot pin oak, but you can look to the future and plant a sapling. You'll need to know how to place it in the landscaping so that it doesn't eat your house, because you know what's really expensive? Tearing out badly placed trees. And no, you can't do that yourself. ☐

Understory trees. These smaller trees like some shade and are great for a front yard. The darlings of the landscape, Japanese maples, are in this group. ☐

Perennials. You want colorful and low maintenance? These babies come back every year. You'll find plants in a wide range of flavors for different locations ~ sun, shade, wet, dry, you name it! ☐

Annuals. A yearly investment, but annuals bring it by blooming all summer (they die with the onset of cold weather). ☐

You can use this list to navigate your way around the departments of a garden center, too, but you'll look like a real dork if you bring along this book. ★ Need help with heavy lifting? Go to Hire a Guy (page 22).

Ground covers. These low-growing creepers are a good way to dress up a large area. They're nicer to look at than bare soil and a little cheaper than other plants, but they aren't super-noticeable until they get established.

Mulch. Are the neighbors mulching? With what? There are more ways to mulch than you could possibly imagine.

Climbers. People use vines in interesting ways. No, not like Tarzan did. Use vines to cover up something you don't want to look at or use them to give you some privacy.

Hardscaping. This includes walks, walls, drives, and patios. Materials can be wood, stone pavers, even gravel. This might seem like the most difficult thing you could do in DIY landscaping, but it isn't.

Accessories. Pots, knickknacks, benches, tables and chairs, and house numbers (and don't forget the gnomes): Who's doing what?

Lighting. Take a stroll in the evening. Lighting is an often overlooked accent that makes a huge difference, but only at night. Why do all this work and leave it in the dark?

Design. Try to think about why things are placed as they are. Is that hedge for privacy or to provide berries for the birds? Is that tree for shade or for blooms? Is that flower color meant to match the doors and shutters??

What's ugly? I think this is just as important as figuring out what you like. What is absolutely hideous? Red mulch? White stone? Overly shaped shrubs? A carnival of striped flowers?

* If you're sure you can handle this on your own, flip to It's All You (page 32).
* Detour: Go to Word Find (page 30) for a fun and informative word hunt, so we can see what you've learned so far.

These Dreams

Now, if you hate your current 'scape, I bet you're wondering why you're drawing up a meticulous map of it. Well, when you're dreaming big, you've got to start someplace.

The next step is to make a bunch of copies of your master plan; put one in your LANDSCAPING file. Now you can use one, or a few, of these copies to create the yard of your dreams (on paper, at least). Just go doodle-tastic on it. Use colored markers and just mess around! I like to use a light green marker for turf, dark green for trees and evergreens, gray for walks, black for the driveway, and crazy colors for annuals and perennials. Draw in a sanctuary for skunks if it pleases you. Do you want a pool someday but you think it will never be in the budget? Draw in a pool. If you want a chocolate fondue fountain in the center of the new circular driveway, add it.

Dream big, ask everyone in your household for ideas, and sleep on it. Heck, you can hibernate on it. Take your time and do it right. (Mr. Rogers taught me that.)

Why not have a cocktail before you draw your dream landscape?

Get your priorities straight. You may win the lottery next month and be able to put in that pool, but if you just poured a cement patio with your children's handprints, you'll be in a tough spot.

If you're overwhelmed or just plain lethargic but have a few ideas you're interested in pursuing, see Where's My Motivation? (page 29) ★ If you're begging for mercy, see Hire a Guy (page 22).

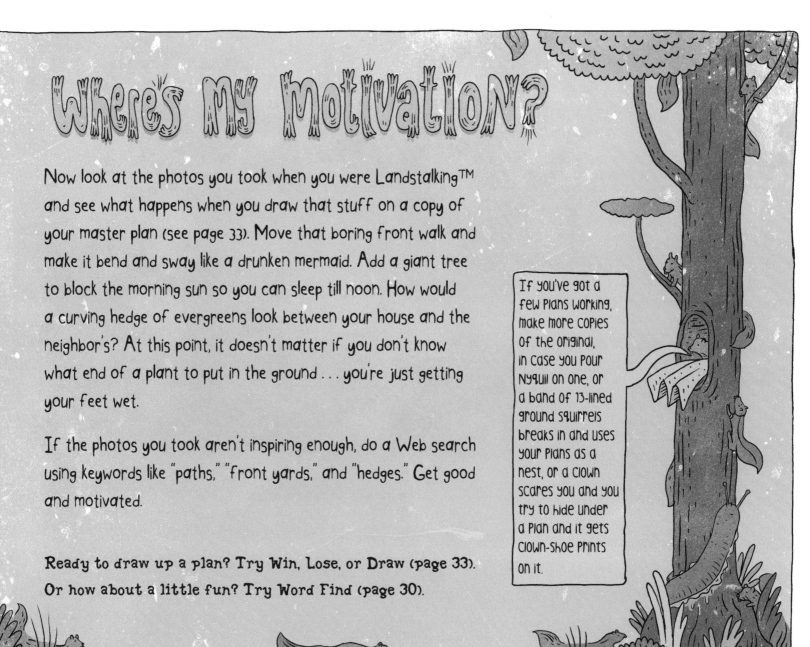

Where's My Motivation?

Now look at the photos you took when you were Landstalking™ and see what happens when you draw that stuff on a copy of your master plan (see page 33). Move that boring front walk and make it bend and sway like a drunken mermaid. Add a giant tree to block the morning sun so you can sleep till noon. How would a curving hedge of evergreens look between your house and the neighbor's? At this point, it doesn't matter if you don't know what end of a plant to put in the ground . . . you're just getting your feet wet.

If the photos you took aren't inspiring enough, do a Web search using keywords like "paths," "front yards," and "hedges." Get good and motivated.

Ready to draw up a plan? Try Win, Lose, or Draw (page 33). Or how about a little fun? Try Word Find (page 30).

If you've got a few plans working, make more copies of the original, in case you pour NyQuil on one, or a band of 13-lined ground squirrels breaks in and uses your plans as a nest, or a clown scares you and you try to hide under a plan and it gets clown-shoe prints on it.

WORD FIND

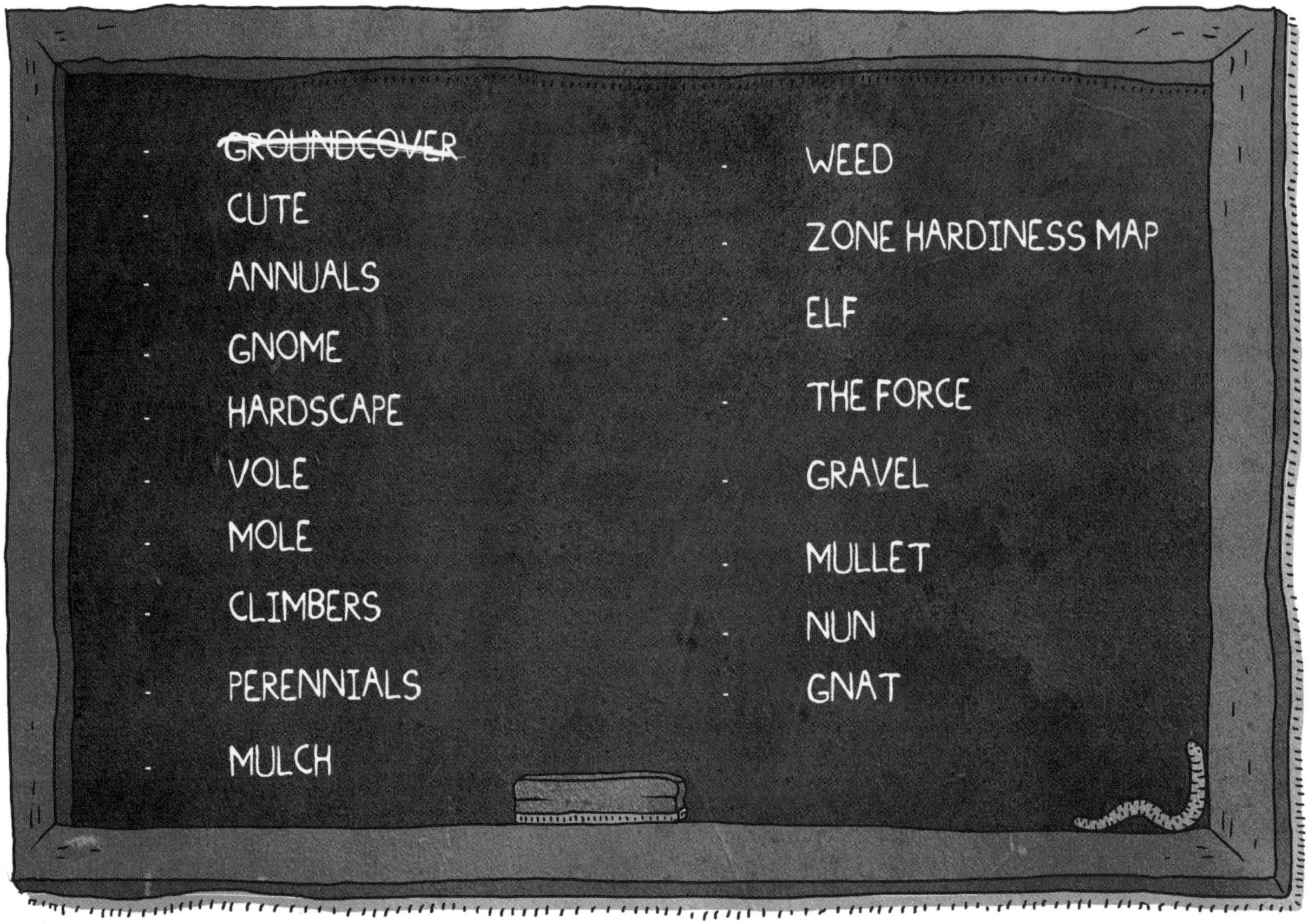

- ~~GROUNDCOVER~~
- CUTE
- ANNUALS
- GNOME
- HARDSCAPE
- VOLE
- MOLE
- CLIMBERS
- PERENNIALS
- MULCH

- WEED
- ZONE HARDINESS MAP
- ELF
- THE FORCE
- GRAVEL
- MULLET
- NUN
- GNAT

L	G	R	O	U	N	D	C	O	V	E	R	C	U	T	E
A	N	N	U	A	L	S	G	N	O	M	E	M	R	T	V
N	O	S	G	O	H	A	R	D	S	C	A	P	E	E	D
D	M	Q	A	H	B	R	R	A	E	D	B	P	A	E	R
S	E	U	R	H	E	U	D	W	S	A	O	L	T	N	G
T	U	I	D	A	A	B	E	R	I	V	W	E	I	N	V
A	N	R	E	Z	S	S	N	U	G	I	I	V	O	L	E
L	I	R	N	E	T	R	I	M	N	D	E	M	O	L	E
K	C	E	C	L	I	M	B	E	R	S	E	W	O	K	N
I	O	L	E	R	E	P	E	R	E	N	N	I	A	L	S
N	R	S	N	M	U	L	C	H	M	T	F	B	W	Y	O
G	N	A	T	G	N	O	M	E	G	N	U	W	E	E	D
Z	O	N	E	H	A	R	D	I	N	E	S	S	M	A	P
E	L	F	R	T	H	O	F	O	R	C	E	B	E	N	N
G	R	A	V	E	L	X	M	U	L	L	E	T	N	U	N

IT'S ALL YOU

After reading all that malarkey, you've chosen to design your own landscape.

The way I see it, either you're cheap or you have control issues. Either way, I admire your spunk! I'm guessing you've taken on projects before, maybe some indoor renovations, or maybe you've dabbled in the outdoor arts and have an inflated idea of your abilities . . .

You can do this, but in the beginning it's going to be a total plan-o-rama. I can admit that the planning is just as painful as the actual physical labor, but at least I'm not asking you to get anything pierced. The first thing is to draw up a landscape plan. It's fine if you're a bad artist; it doesn't matter if you can't even draw a straight line. If you can count, you'll be okay. I swear. If you can't count, ask a grade school kid to help.

Scared? You should be. Turn to Vive la Différence! (page 38).

Now is probably a good time to say this: There's a chance that you can't do it yourself. I know I just said you could, but I don't want to candy-coat things. I don't know you. Design is one of those things, well, either you have it or you don't. Can you dress yourself? Do you own decorative pillows? Well, those are steps in the right direction. Have a friend with better taste than yours? Maybe a friend with a green thumb? What about a friend who's just plain bossy? Now is the time to invite them over for beers.

To learn how to draw up a landscape plan, go to Win, Lose, or Draw (page 33).
Flip to Hire a Guy (page 22) if you give up already.

WIN, LOSE, OR DRAW

The first step to A Master Plan is to make a drawing of your area-in-question. Does that sound dirty? I didn't mean it to (this time).

There are a few ways you can do this. The easiest is to see if there are any plot plans or architect's drawings that came with your house when you bought it. If that's not going to happen, thankfully technology has made it a little less strenuous than it used to be to draw your own.

Get yourself some graph paper (you can buy it anywhere) and park yourself at a computer. Check out the view of your own house from either Google Maps or Google Earth. Print the photo of your property and trace it, to the best of your ability, onto the graph paper. I've found that placing the map under a piece of the paper and then holding them up against a sunny window and tracing with a pencil serves as a poor man's light box.

Mark property lines, tree placement, and where your house is. Do the best you can.

Google Maps is a cinch to use: Look up your address, then print the map of your yard. Google Earth is a little trickier (you have to download the program), but once you have it, you can actually use it to measure your outer space — right there from outer space.

Flip to Walk It Off (page 34) if you think your plan is good enough. I'll be nurturing and tell you to read this page over again if your plan stinks. If you need help, slink on over to *Vive la Différence!* (page 38).

If Google Maps is too difficult for you, another way to get a great aerial view is to go skydiving in your neighborhood with a sketchpad and pencil in hand.

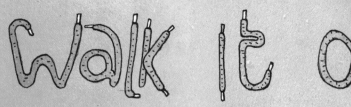

Walk it off

Now it's time to measure stuff, with a legit measuring device, such as a measuring wheel or measuring tape. Accuracy is king. Remember the scene from *This Is Spinal Tap,* where they make Stonehenge 18 inches instead of 18 feet? You don't want that to be you. The goal is to get every detail of your existing landscape: every plant, brick, ant, and squirrel.

Start by measuring from your house to the street, then your house to the walk, the driveway to the fence, the fence to the house. There's no such thing as overkill. If there's an enormous tree in the front yard, measure from the house to the tree, the street to the tree, the fence to the tree, the fire hydrant to the tree, the tree to the sun. Even if you used Google Earth or an architect's plan, make sure this is ultra-precise.

Don't forget to draw in any large tree canopies that shade your property, whether it be on your land or coming over from a neighbor's.

Walk it off: Want to learn how to measure an area without the help of an actual measuring device? Well, you need one to start. Measure your foot. Is it anywhere near 12 inches long? If it is, just walk, heel to toe, around any space and count your steps. If your feet are too tiny or too big for that business, practice taking 3-foot-long (1-yard) strides, measured at first until you get good, and count those. I look dumb doing it (and so will you), but it always works.

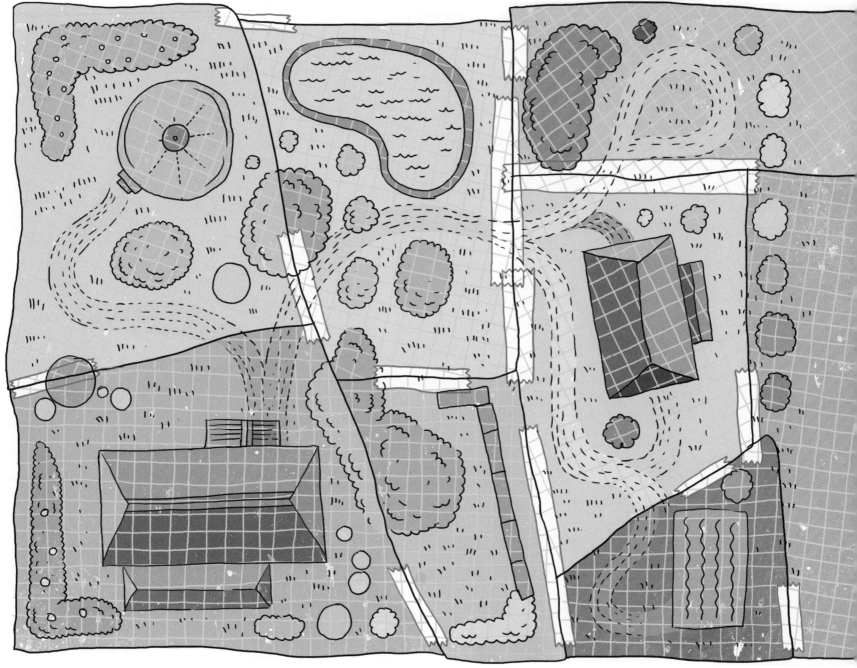

You swore there wouldn't be math

I lied.

You'll need a little math to figure out how to scale this on your graph paper. Will each square represent 1 foot? 5 feet? Be wary of going too small ~ for example, using one square to mean 20 feet. I like 1:5 or 1:10. Better to keep it simple and use several sheets, taped together or individually for each area. Also, drawing your plan on as many pieces of paper as you need helps you break down projects into manageable pieces. A word to the smarty-pants: Don't bring a giant taped-together plan into a garden center for free advice. The staff will run screaming.

I thought I was hot snot and tried to squeeze too much into a plan. Everything was so tiny that the result was a hot mess. So don't do it.

Did I mention
you should use a pencil for this?
I didn't? I should have.
About six pages ago.

Was math the turning point?
Are you crying uncle?
Turn to Hire a Guy (page 22).

If you've been bolstered by a grandiose ego and want to keep dreaming, turn to These Dreams (page 28).

Vive la Différence!

If you want someone to give you a ton of ideas, draw up a plan, and then take your money, you need a landscape architect or a garden designer. Which would be better for you? These are generalizations, but here's a brief description of each:

A landscape architect (LA) went to school for many years and knows all things architectural. Many, however, don't know much about plants. If you have tricky drainage issues, a priceless or historic home, a complicated site, or money to burn, an LA is the way to go. Before you go about hiring, find spaces you like and ask who designed them. You'll have to decide whether to choose an established and experienced LA or an up-and-comer with fresh ideas. Either will measure your space within an inch of its life; accuracy is their strength. You will pay for this accuracy, through the wazoo. The cost will compare with having an architect draw up plans for a home.

A garden designer (GD) probably didn't go to school for outdoor-space planning, but may have taken a course or two. Many are simply excellent gardeners who were told "Hey, I'll pay you to do this for me" over and over and over. Typically, they know plants, and charge a whole lot less than an LA will. You won't get the same extent of planning — usually a quick pencil sketch on graph paper, although sometimes a full plan. If you want to hire a GD, ask around, as you would for an LA, and, for that matter, anyone else you want to hire for any other kind of job.

Meet with several candidates.
Make sure you ask if there'll be an initial fee when you set up the first appointment. You can expect the person you choose to poke around your outdoor space. She'll want to go inside your house, too, to determine your tastes and see how you live. That person will be hanging out at your house a lot in the future, so go with the one you like most. It's essential that you really, really like her or him.

You can check out websites to see candidates' work, but anyone can airbrush, and, even worse, anyone can steal a photo off the Internet and post it as his own work. I highly recommend you see those gardens *for real:* It shouldn't be that difficult, as you're bound to hire someone local.

How to spot a PHONY Landscape Architect

Are you pretty sure he's making up those Latin plant names?

AH YES... PETUNIAOBLONGATA

Look for fake moustaches.

A landscape architect will work the fact that she is, indeed, an architect into any conversation at least three times.

High heels scream "PHONY!"

Is he wearing perfume/cologne? Outdoorsy people smell of the earth.

Is he wearing white? That's bad.

Want to know more about the options? Go immediately to Help! I Need Somebody (page 74). Already Hired a Guy? Turn to The Labor Party (page 50).

You Can't Always Get What You Want...

You know you want an evergreen hedge for privacy but you have no idea what kind of evergreen or how many you need, or how close to plant them so your neighbors can't see that in summer you hang your panties on the line to dry.

You know you want a perennial bed with plants that are low maintenance and bloom for most of the summer.

You know you want something to go in that corner that won't attract bees, 'cause you're allergic.

You want to make a garden in a shady spot where it seems like nothing will grow.

How are you going to figure out the answers? I thought about including my phone number in this book. I mean, I'm very grateful you bought the dang thing, but with time zones and the fact that I need at least 13 hours of beauty sleep to be even remotely palatable, I've decided to keep my digits on the DL.

Which means even *more* work for you. You'll have to think deeply about what attributes you're looking for, write them down, grab the car keys, and I'll meet you at the garden center. But if I'm late, go ahead: Ask one of the knowledgeable employees for help.

So, write down optimal heights and widths for each space you're thinking about. Jot down times when you need them to look their most fabulous (Do they need to be evergreen? Do you want them to bloom red for Bastille Day?). Note the sun exposure and the soil situation, too (see Soil, Yourself, page 62).

An area is considered to be in full sun if it gets more than 6 hours of sun a day, partly sunny if it gets between 4 and 6 hours a day, and shady if less than 4 hours daily.

Observe a space for a day to see if it is what you think it is.

Set a timer and check the area every hour. Tons of people are surprised by what they see. Maybe someone will invent an app to tell you your sun exposure.

OH, just do me a favor and flip to the next stinkin' page already!

BUT if YOU TRY, SOMETIMES YOU GET WHAT YOU NEED

Take the list of what you need – or what you think you need – to the nursery. With just some of the specifics, you'll be able to tap in to some golden info. If you're able to say "I need a tall tree that doesn't get more than thirteen feet wide and doesn't mind wet soil" or "I need an evergreen shrub that I can prune into a hedge" or "I need a long-blooming perennial that requires no care at all, and it has to be orange," you're giving enough information to get some back. If you just stroll in and say "I need a tree,"

no one will know where to start. In fact, you'll make enemies, and a secret code will be announced over the loudspeaker system to alert someone to let the air out of your tires before you get back to the parking lot.

Feel free to take a bite-size piece of your drawing into the garden center, too. Ask that helpful employee what she thinks of your plan. Ask what she'd plant. You'll be amazed at how passionately the right person will give advice. If you get the wrong person — someone who knows nothing, who was hired to do the watering — or if you accidentally ask another customer, keep trying.

If you did this part and you have a professionally approved list of plants, you're golden. Now flip back to So, You Think You Can Plant (page 17).

If you're befuddled, do more research. Turn to Tree to Be You and Me (page 73), or to Shrubs: The Khaki Pants of the Landscape (page 79).

Or think about the pretties by checking out Forever Yours, Perennials (page 119). I'll expect a report on my desk in the morning.

~TIPS GALORE~

Here are some more design tips to ponder:

Taller homes need taller trees and plants to "anchor" them. It turns out that homes don't like to be the tallest person in the room. This is called scale. And we'll talk about it a lot more later on down the road.

Evergreens are vital, vital, vital in climates with winter because once all the other plants lose their leaves in autumn, the shrubs with needles and evergreen leaves are all you have to look at. Evergreens keep me on this side of the thin line between getting up every morning and sheer insanity. So, big thanks to the spruce in my front yard!

Repetition is important, to draw everything together. Repetition is important, to draw everything together.
There are many ways to accomplish this: for example, use the same kinds of plants; use groups of plants that are similar in height, color, or texture; echo a theme; utilize hardscaping in similar ways around the yard.

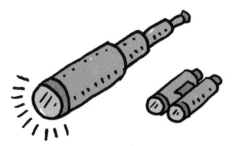

Make sure you change up your perspective when you're designing. Don't look from only one spot: Check it out from inside the house, from all windows and every level; view from the street and from the neighbors' yard. For fun, take a gander from the neighbors' guest bathroom when they aren't home.

When designing, start from the biggest elements and work down to the smallest. In other words, first the big trees, last the ground covers.

Form is great, but a lot of design is also about repetition. Does your house have a pointy roof? What about a rounded bay window? Is everything about your house boxy? Well, then, consider repeating that roof with pyramidal plants, add roundy-moundy shrubs to accent the window, add something that enjoys being squarish, like a prunable boxwood (get it? BOXwood!) or a yew to pick up on the house's boxiness.

Color: It's the word you've been waiting for.

Instead of getting all your color from annuals and perennials, look for ways to incorporate it throughout your landscaping. There are blooming trees and shrubs, and plants with wildly variegated leaves, leaves of dark purple. There's room for shakin' it up all over the place.

Hey, Tool

There's a tool for every job. Most are easy to find and inexpensive.
Some~like a compactor and an aerator~ are fun power tools you can rent for the day.
Can you match the tool to the project?

Tool		Project
Shovel		Smoothing out anything from grass seed to chunky materials like gravel, diamonds, and gnome poop
Stump grinder		Stirring up old soil to make it easier to plant
Rock rake		Removing material like soil, pirate booty, and miniature pony manure (and also adding it)
Pruners		Pretty much every project you can think of, at the very least, it makes a great drink cooler
Rototiller		Removing a large tree from the yard, roots intact, in minutes, at great expense
Wheelbarrow		Poking holes in the lawn to relieve compaction and enable better water infiltration
45-inch tree spade		Putting in fence poles, yo
Seed spreader		Shaping trees and deadheading
One-man auger		For when you've removed a giant tree and have something left to remind you of it
Aerator		Spreading grass seed or fertilizer at a measured rate

Lots of garden centers will deliver and plant a tree for you for a minimal fee. I encourage you to take advantage of that. They're going to do it better and faster than you ever could.

Even big-box hardware stores rent big tools

Answer Key: *Shovel* = Removing material like soil, pirate booty, and miniature pony manure (and also adding it); *Stump grinder* = For when you've removed a giant tree and have something left to remind you of it; *Rock rake* = Smoothing out anything from grass seed to chunky materials like gravel, diamonds, and gnome poop; *Pruners* = Shaping trees and deadheading; *Rototiller* = Stirring up old soil to make it easier to plant; *Wheelbarrow* = Pretty much every project you can think of; at the very least, it makes a great drink cooler; *Tree spade* = Removing a large tree from the yard, roots intact, in minutes, at great expense; *Seed spreader* = Spreading grass seed or fertilizer at a measured rate; *One-man auger* = Putting in fence poles, yo; *Aerator* = Poking holes in the lawn to relieve compaction and enable better water infiltration

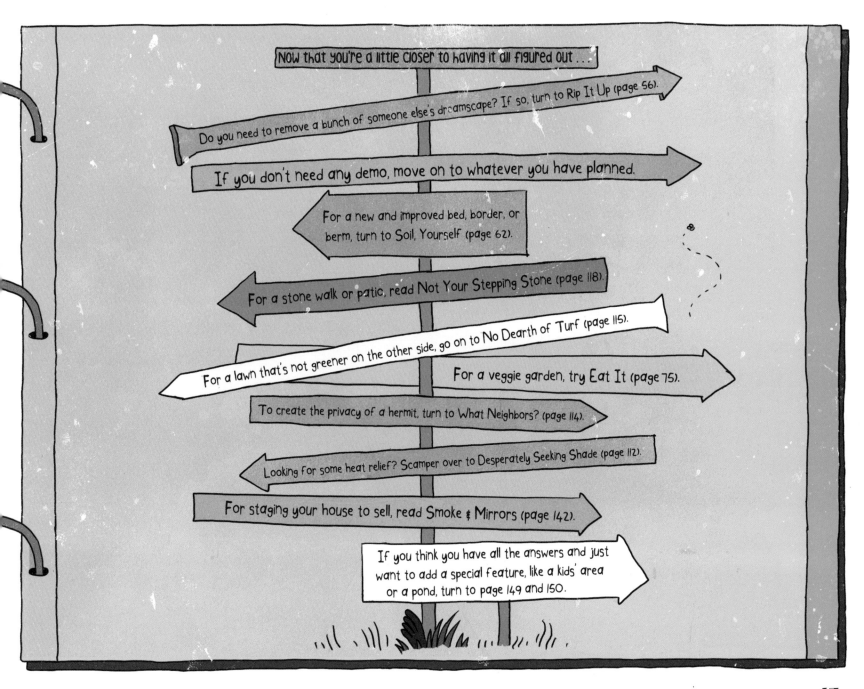

Now that you're a little closer to having it all figured out . . .

Do you need to remove a bunch of someone else's dreamscape? If so, turn to Rip It Up (page 56).

If you don't need any demo, move on to whatever you have planned.

For a new and improved bed, border, or berm, turn to Soil, Yourself (page 62).

For a stone walk or patio, read Not Your Stepping Stone (page 118).

For a lawn that's not greener on the other side, go on to No Dearth of Turf (page 115).

For a veggie garden, try Eat It (page 75).

To create the privacy of a hermit, turn to What Neighbors? (page 114).

Looking for some heat relief? Scamper over to Desperately Seeking Shade (page 112).

For staging your house to sell, read Smoke & Mirrors (page 142).

If you think you have all the answers and just want to add a special feature, like a kids' area or a pond, turn to page 149 and 150.

Born Tree?

Some things are free! Go get some! Here are some possibilities:

Topsoil and mulch

Many municipalities offer free compost or free mulch. You have to schlep it yourself, but it's free. Some places will deliver for a small fee. Similarly, these municipal compost and mulch sites will usually take away yard waste, including leaves, tree limbs, and grass clippings. Learn more about debris in Tear It Up (page 64) and about composting your own darn yard waste in Compostest Is the Mostest (page 70).

Tree work

Is your giant tree rubbing some power lines the wrong way? You may be able to get people from the power company to come and prune it, or even remove it. But be careful what you wish for;

they usually do a crappy job. Maybe they'll hack away limbs that are crucial to the structure of the tree, or they'll just make it look really ugly.

Leaves

In autumn, I go around the neighborhood and steal bags of leaves to use as mulch or to add to the compost heap.

Labor and materials

Check Craigslist for free materials; I often see stone mentioned there. If you have something in your yard you want to be rid of but it's too big of a pain in the neck to do it yourself, put it on Freecycle as "Free ditch lilies: you dig." It'll get the job done and you don't even have to be home when it happens.

FREE!

DECKS IN THE CITY

Treat your deck as you would any other room of your house that it rains in. But you should be able to use it as a living space, for sure. What will it take for that to be possible? Here's what's what:

Furniture. A table and chairs to eat on? Some loungers to bask on? A tiki bar? A hammock? There's is an amazing range of patio furniture out there, and some of it doesn't look like outdoor stuff. Be sure to look for weather-resistant fabrics, if you go the upholstered route. Buy only what you know you'll use. If the thought of eating outside makes you itch, skip the table.

Containers. If it's a few pots here and there, built-in boxes, or baskets hanging from the rails, flowers really soften up the place! Make sure to check out Drip It Good (page 131), if you want to set it up yourself, or read Hire a Guy (page 22) to get someone to do it for you.

If you think you're going to water every day when you get home from work, your plants and I laugh at you.

Heat. They make rad patio heaters now, so you can enjoy your space a little earlier and also extend the season. Feeling industrious? Go for a full fireplace out there, too. Or stop at the garden center and pick up a metal fire pit, or even one of those clay chimeneas.

Lighting. You're going to want lights out there, so check out page 146 for ideas on how to install them yourself or page 38 to find out how to get somebody to have all your ideas for you. Or you could just string up chile-pepper lights. Keep it classy, yo.

Mosquitoes can make things unbearable for most of the summer. Why not try a pop-up screen tent? And in addition to the usual sprays and candles, or maybe instead, you can pay bats to hang out and eat mosquitoes all night long.

What else can you have? A hot tub, ceiling fan, full kitchen, beer bong, TV, water features, a half pipe, grill, and outdoor rugs.

Now would be a great time to check out Annual Means Always Having to Say Goodbye (page 102), if you haven't already.

Or flip to Smoke & Mirrors (page 142).

DETOUR: For low-budget deckscaping ideas, turn to Hobo Deck Style (page 84).

Be aware that where there are flowers, there are bees.

The Labor Party

There is nothing like having 15 guys show up at your house and paying them to do stuff you don't want to do; it feels great. When choosing a company, do your homework:

* It should have a nice truck with the name of the company and its phone number painted on the side. Magnets, address labels, and duct tape are bad signs.

* Make sure employees are licensed and bonded.

* I like a company with a website; that's just me.

* Your contact should speak English (unless you can speak their native language), should understand your needs and wants, and offer solutions to problems.

* It's critical that you get an estimate for services. If you're offered the option of paying for T&M (that means time and materials) until the end of the job, you could get gouged. If you go contract, which means you agree to the quoted price ahead of time, make sure you know exactly what's on it and what it all means.

* If you're hiring for a weekly mow and blow (lawn and leaves, that is), meet with someone to go over your expectations. For example, you can ask the crew to come on Fridays because you party all weekend. You can tell them never to come after 1 pm because your kid naps and the blowers will wake him. You can ask for them to come on Wednesdays, so they can bring the recycling bins into the garage. Think it through.

* Don't ask a mow-and-blow crew to, say, remove a tree that fell in a storm. Or to bury a pet. Or to clean out your garage. Or your gutters. Those are all services they may be able to perform for you, but they have a schedule to adhere to. If you want something special, call the company and get it lined up.

A maintenance crew may not be who you want to, say, prune your prizewinning roses. Or pinch back your asters. For that, you may want a real-life gardener. Doesn't that sound snobby? Oh, well. Turn to Help! I Need Somebody (page 74) for details.

Man, that's a lot of info. Take a day off before checking out Where's My Hose? (page 55) to learn about irrigation.

Don't need irrigation? Everyone could use a little outdoor lighting, so turn to This Little Light of Mine (page 58) instead.

KISS MY ASTer GUIDE to GARDEN FASHION

Watering, Weeding & Deadheading

Demolition, Digging & Planting

Martini

Lipstick

Miniskirt

Gardening gloves

Bare legs

Rake

Flip-flops

Giant sun hat

Old T-shirt

Cargo pants

Steel-toed shoes

You know what you can't do?

Anything that involves big trees.
Don't even think about it.
Instead, call a reputable tree guy when:

* You think you have an insect or disease problem, like emerald ash borer or some kind of badass fungus.

* You want some tree limbs removed because they've died, or because you want to let in some sun for the beds underneath, or because you want to change the size or shape of the tree.

* You want a tall tree removed.

* You've got storm damage.

* You want to dig up a big tree to transplant. One of you will die, either the tree or you. It could really go either way.

* Look for an established company that doesn't get too chain-saw-happy. Make sure employees are licensed and bonded. Ask if the company has a tree spade (a giant circular shovel on the back of a truck; it takes minutes to dig out a tree, but at a spendy price), if it does stump grinding, if there's a cherry picker. If the company has all that equipment, probably no one's doing any high jinks with a tightrope and a chain saw.

* A reputable tree guy is apparent the second you start to speak with him. You want someone who loves trees. He should give off a very "Lorax" vibe.

Learn more about trees at Tree to Be You and Me (Page 73).
Read about tearing out stuff at TEAR It Up (Page 64).

Dear Amanda

Sometimes things go up in flames and you don't know why. Here are a few questions I've received from my imaginary readers:

Dear Amanda,

I used a spray-on fertilizer the other day and figured, "Hey, if some is good, more must be better!" Soon after, I noticed scorched splotches on my plants. What happened?

Sincerely,
Scorched in Seattle

Ouch! Remember: Chemical fertilizers are, yes, chemicals, and therefore able to burn, baby, burn. Do us both a favor and strictly follow the directions on the box or bag. Or use milder organic fertilizers (page 148). And still follow the directions.

Dear Amanda,

I put down a fresh batch of mulch recently, and everything went to crap. My yard looks like all the green has been sucked out of it!

Yours, Yellow in Amarillo

Whoa, I bet your mulch wasn't aged. Therefore, as it aged "on the job," it stole all the nitrogen you had going on. Make sure you always use composted or aged materials (page 70).

Dear Amanda,

I put all my plants in the ground, kept them watered, and they still festered and died. I'm so sad. What should I do?
Perplexed in Philly

Hmm. Is there a black walnut tree nearby? Black walnuts make poison (called jugione) in every part of their body — leaves, fruit, bark, roots. To add insult to injury, that poison can extend more than 50 feet from the tree's trunk, if it's feeling up to it. You're pretty much DOOMED.

There are a few plants that tolerate jugione, but you'll have to do some homework on that.

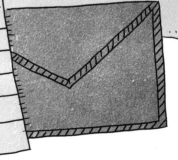

DROPPING ACID (OR ALKALINITY)

For this one, you really have to get a soil test. This consists of digging up some soil, putting it in a resealable sandwich baggie, and sending it off to a lab for analysis. Technicians there will then let you know what sort of soil you have and what to do to fix it.

Most plants like a pH (the measurement of acidity or alkalinity) between 6.0 and 7.5. If your soil is more alkaline, be prepared to add aluminum sulfate, sphagnum peat, or iron sulfate to lower the pH. Follow the directions on the container (these amendments are available at any garden center). If your soil is more acid than you want it to be, you'll need to raise your pH. I'd try laying on the compost before doing anything else, because compost will slowly raise the pH and it's hard to have too much of it. If you try to correct the pH by adding lime, you can easily add too much of the stuff and bungle it to a point that's hard to recover from.

To learn how to **fix other soil** problems, check out Soil-Change Operation (page 66) ∼ AND ∼ Compostest Is the Mostest (page 70).

A little goes a long way, and it takes a long time to get there. Years, even.

You can find out where to get your soil tested by checking with your local extension office, or by Googling "soil test" and the state you live in. Or you can find one by shining a bat-shaped light into the sky.

54

Where's My Hose?

If you're going to spend money on plants and you know you're too lazy to water them with consistency, do yourself a favor and get an irrigation system. If you have a small garden or live somewhere that gets a lot of rain during the growing season, you can probably hack it without one (if you promise to use Outlook to schedule regular watering reminders). This can mean putting in pop-up heads all over the lawn, so your yard looks like a mini-golf course. Or it could mean putting in a small drip-irrigation system (page 131) that waters your containers or vegetable garden. Ask friends (assuming you have some) who have grown-up irrigation, and if they'd recommend the company that installed it.

Usually, there isn't much emotional involvement in choosing an irrigation company; it's not exactly an aesthetic field. When you come down to it, either a crew comes when you call or doesn't. After installation, you can count on your company to get you started every spring and turn off the system every fall. Request that the timer be located someplace easily accessible so you don't need to be home for them to service it.

There's more info about irrigation in Less Irritation through Irrigation (page 134). You'd rather talk about electricity (as it pairs *so* well with water)? Turn to This Little Light of Mine (page 58).

RIP IT UP

Tearing out is so much fun that I almost want to come over and help you. Almost. Let's not get crazy here, though. What are you tearing out? If you're creating a lot of landscape waste and you're not composting it (check out Compostest Is the Mostest, page 70), be sure you're ditching it in a way that's responsible and legal. In some areas, there's a fee for curbside leaf and debris pickup. Some towns have a composting facility you can bring garden waste to. Perhaps you can compost some of it but not all. Consider a dumpster bag from your trash-collection company. This is like a giant IKEA bag. The company drops it off, you fill it with crap, then you give a call to say, "Come and get it."

There are places that recycle concrete and asphalt as well. As for old lumber, try to reuse it, but if that doesn't work, how about a bonfire? Just make sure what you're burning is safe; some lumber is pressure treated, and, man, you don't want *those* fumes in your lungs! Oh, and check with the fire department — some places have restrictions (especially if you live in the fire-prone West).

You gonna keep ripping it up? Turn to Tear It Up (page 64).

Want a soil-improvement regimen? You're ready for Soil, Yourself (page 62).

Getting rid of plants you don't like but are alive? Why not offer them for free on Craigslist to improve your Craigslist karma?

HEDGE FUND(S)

I bet you want a hedge.

Way to start out easy, chief.

A hedge is a series of the same shrub (often boxwood or yew), lined up and planted close together and then pruned to look like one continuous plant.

Everyone seems to want one, even though it's endlessly labor-intensive, you have to buy A TON of plants to start, and then you have to prune it correctly (and religiously), often using stakes and twine and a level. Do I have to go on, or can you envision the horrors?

How about a ton of flowers instead? Or a few nice rows of broccoli . . .

Hedges are sometimes planted with barberry. Watch out! It's deceptively prickly and also on some lists of invasive species. And it has been known to let the air out of people's tires.

Dogs are the mortal enemy of boxwood. One drop of pee can do a ton of damage.

THIS LITTLE LIGHT OF MINE

Well-lit landscaping is a pleasure to behold, especially if you live in a climate that "celebrates" winter. Besides, an uplight on a tall tree, a wash against a wall ... they're nice to come home to. Here are two routes to take:

SPENDY.

I like a landscape lighting company that specializes in what it does — it should concentrate on landscape lighting and not also be a dry-cleaning delivery service or do vending-machine repair. I want actual electricians playing with the wires around my home. Find a couple of companies online (or from recommendations), give them a call, and ask for some addresses you can drive by at night to check out their work. Have someone from each company come to your house and give you all her ideas and write them down for you, so you can pick and choose, buffet style. Find out how easy it would be to add some features later, and let that help guide your decision making.

CHEAP

What? You're too cheap/poor? There are solar path lights just about everywhere you look. There are always twinkle/Christmas lights, tiki torches, and luminaria, too.

Think you might need a garden coach? Turn to Help! I Need Somebody (page 74). Are you too cool for that? Maybe you'll be interested in Born Free (page 48), about getting stuff for nothing.

lighting
DOs & DON'Ts

DO
use lighting
that's
different
from the
neighbors'

DON'T
jar up
hundreds
of lightning
bugs

 DO
think about
going solar

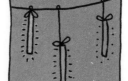

DON'T
string up
glow sticks

 DO
use a timer
so that you're
not lighting
up the wee
hours after
everyone's
gone to bed

DON'T
nail lights
into your trees.
Poor trees ...

Ferns, Moss & evergreens

If you live someplace where winter takes over for what seems like forever, evergreens can make the difference between sanity and going Cocoa Puffs. You say you don't really "do" winter? They're still a wise design option because some of them introduce totally different textures into the garden mix. Most evergreens are needled conifers (meaning "cone-bearing"), but some, like holly, live oak, and boxwood, have broad leaves. Evergreens, much like St. Bernard puppies, start off cute and manageable and then become giants in the blink of an eye, so it's incredibly important that you know their mature height and spread before you bring them home. Here are some good choices.

Dwarf Alberta spruce.
This conical little kid is slow-growing and great for a container. Whenever I see a row of them, topping out at 4 feet, separating two driveways, I weep a conical tear.

Boxwood.
I think it's overused, but people seem to love it. And it does do some things that are special: the best thing is that it'll grow in shade. It also makes a great hedge or it can be sculpted over time to resemble the San Diego Chicken or Mr. T.

Chamaecyparis.
This is Latin for "perfect-size evergreen." In this family you'll find all sorts of awesome options for a backyard, from small shaggy yellow shrubs that remind me of Clyde from Pac Man to trees that look like a bonsai that got out of hand.

Dwarf mugo pine.
This is a dicey one, because it's often mislabeled. If it's small and cute when you buy it and then devours your house, oops, wrong tree. Get a true dwarf mugo from a reputable nursery and enjoy!

Evergreens come in a number of shapes: pyramid, cone, globe, tufty spreader, and creepy creeper. Stop thinking "Christmas tree."

Holly. Where I live, outside Chicago, everything is all wrong for holly — the climate, the soil, the hairstyles, but mostly the (lack of) drainage. So if you have great drainage and you don't live on the ice planet Hoth, grow ahead! I salute you. Keep in mind that for most berried hollies, you need a dude and a lady plant. You dig?

Arborvitae. This is usually a tall, narrow shrub that when massed provides great privacy. (See What Neighbors? page 114) It's tough as nails and does pretty well in a container, too. For another use, see Decks in the City (page 49).

Yew. This shrub is often inherited with an older home. The heirs always hate it, but it's usually the most appropriate-for-the-period-of-your-house, tough, and low-maintenance thing you can have. The nicest thing about a yew? You can chop it low and it will fill back in from the inside. Most evergreens can't (or won't!) do that.

So what's going under those evergreens?

See Forever Yours, Perennials (page 119).

Go to Annual Means Always Having to Say Goodbye (page 102).

How about mulching? Read Still Life with Mulch (page 125).

Arborvitae = *Thuja* species. Boxwood = *Buxus* species. Chamaecyparis = *Chamaecyparis* species. Dwarf Alberta spruce = *Picea glauca* 'Conica'. Dwarf mugo pine = *Pinus mugo* var. *pumilo*, holly = *Ilex* species. Juniper = *Juniperus* species. Yew = *Taxus* species

Juniper. As tough as it is ugly. It comes coarse and upright and coarse and creeping all over the damn place. Prickly and smells like gin.

SOIL, YOURSELF

You probably think of soil as just what you dig up and bury your plants with. Hells no! It's the key to this whole candy store, yo. If you have crap soil, you can kiss whatever investment you have planted in your yard goodbye. And it's a *Titanic* sort of good-bye. And you just thought it was dirt.

First, do you know what kind of soil you have? There are four kinds — sandy, silty, clay, and loamy — but there are many wackadoo combinations.

Sandy. Sandy soil is easy to identify. If your soil feels in any way gritty, it's got sand in it. If your soil is super sandy, you have a whole other book of issues, like gardening in a desert. However, this also means you have great drainage.

Silty. Silty soil is slippery to the touch. It's not a bad soil, as it's somewhere between the two tough ones to deal with: sand and clay. However, no one gardens in just silt. It's always a mix.

Clay. Clay soil is thick and gummy, much like that stuff you played with in art class. In fact, it could be the same thing, depending on where you live. It may be so thick (even though the particles themselves are teensy) that if you leave the hose on, you end up with a lake. Water has *that* difficult a time getting through. In prolonged heat, it's like pottery.

Loamy. Loamy soil is a combination of the other three soils, and makes for a perfect soil scenario. It almost never happens. When it does, you have nothing to complain about.

DRAINAGE

good

bad

Drainage refers to the rate at which water flows away from a plant's roots.
If it rains and your plants are thirsty 15 minutes later, you have great
drainage. If a puddle forms that lasts for 48 hours, that's not just bad drainage;
your plants had better enjoy "wet feet" (meaning they don't mind their
roots sitting in a bit of water from time to time).

You couldn't care less about soil? Scoot over to Tree to Be You and Me (Page 73) ✱ Want to learn how to change your soil type?
I thought so. Go immediately to Soil-Change Operation (Page 66), please.

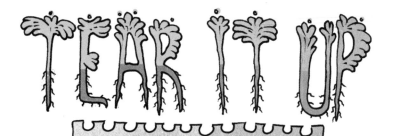

TEAR IT UP

DEMOLITION DOs AND DON'Ts

DON'T film it, just in case there is a future lawsuit. Save yourself.

DO have a plan before you attack

DON'T attach anything to the bumper of anything

DON'T use explosives

DO go slow and use your head

DO wear protective (and fabulous) eyewear

DON'T use gas and a match

DO consider the weight of a dumpster on your driveway before you put one there

DON'T let the kids and dog help

Promise me you won't use a chain attached to the bumper of your car to tear out shrubs.
PROMISE ME.

To remove asphalt or concrete, you'll have to rent a jackhammer. Make sure to get noise-killing headphones and safety glasses while you're at it. Aside from the frenetic action of the jackhammer, the task goes quickly and you won't be sorry you rented one.

If you want to get rid of a big tree, flip to One, Two, Tree (page 52) for why you're probably wrong thinking you can do it yourself.

Itching to yank 60 years' worth of old yews from in front of the house? Consider pruning away a portion of each so you can get at the trunks, then hit those babies with a Sawzall before they know what's happening. Now it'll be easier to dig out the roots with a sharp shovel.

If you want to remove stone that someone used as mulch in the '80s, go to Born Free (page 48) to learn how to trick someone into doing it for you. If that doesn't work, get yourself a rock rake and fill a wheelbarrow with small, manageable loads.

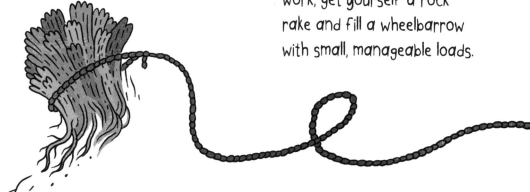

What to do with them now? I suggest throwing them, one at a time over several years, into your least favorite neighbor's yard. Or bury them somewhere on your property, or find a ditch and dump 'em in. Let this be a lesson to those who think stones as mulch is such a rad idea. You can't get rid of them once they go hideously out of fashion.

Lava rock, white chipped gravel, and white round stones have had their moment in the sun, so to speak. In the late '70s and early '80s, they were all the rage. Now they give me rage. They look terrible unless used with total irony, and I rarely see good irony in the home landscape. Stick to natural colors and things that are locally sourced: Check out Can You Hear the Sustainability? (page 122).

Want to get rid of a stump? Call a tree guy (One, Two, Tree, page 52) or rent a stump grinder and go to town!

It'll take less than an hour, unless you're cutting down a redwood, and: don't . . . cut . . . down . . . a . . . redwood.

You've removed everything without hurting yourself, your house, or your neighbors' house and you're ready for the main event.

* What was that again? To make your beds and **not** lie in them, turn to Soil, Yourself (page 62).

* How about a nice stone walk? Go to Not Your Stepping Stone (page 118).

* Or are you looking for a lush, green lawn? Turn back to No Dearth of Turf (page 115).

* Hate your neighbors? Zip off to What Neighbors? (page 114).

* Looking for a shady spot? Go to Desperately Seeking Shade (page 112).

* To get your veggies, flip to Eat It (page 75).

I hate safety. I like to live on the wild side. But not when I'm ripping out stuff. That's when I haul out the steel-toed boots, safety glasses, gloves, and suits of armor for the neighborhood dogs.

SOIL-CHANGE OPERATION

Okay, your soil has way too much clay in it. Your stuff will grow like a Ping-Pong game in space. That is . . . badly.

Dig a gigantic hole for everything you plant (heap up the soil as you dig). Then, after you set the plant in the hole, fill it with a 50/50 mix of good compost or composted manure and the stuff from the pile. When you're digging, be sure the sides of the hole aren't shiny. That's a sign the roots may not be able to break through. Rough up the walls with a pitchfork. Admit it — you've always wanted an excuse to use a pitchfork. To amend an entire bed, remove lots of the clay, loosen some that

remains, and mix in good organic material. Eventually, the clay will break down and become more manageable . . . just in time for your grandkids to enjoy it. If you have the muscles, patience, and cash (my favorite combination), remove all the clay in a planting area and replace it with soil that's loose and flowy.

If you're really having a hard time, mail a soil sample to a lab and the folks there will send you back the barely readable results of their analysis. It will tell you what kind of soil you have and what you should do to it to make it awesome.

You can't know enough about soil.

To learn about sandy soil, go to Sandy Handy (page 70).

To become a pro at composting (which is mandatory), check out Compostest Is the Mostest (page 70).

Enough with the soil science? Flip to Soil, Yourself (page 62), and then wash your hands.

MOST plantings fail because of crap soil. Amend, my friend.

To B&B or not to B&B.

Trees and shrubs come balled and burlapped (a.k.a. B&B), in a container, *or bareroot.*

Balled and burlapped

is a term used for trees that have been nursery grown (in rows), dug up (either by hand or with a machine called a tree spade), then have had their roots and the surrounding soil wrapped with burlap and tied with twine. Most big trees come this way.

Container-grown trees

are exactly that — trees in pots. They're nice because most likely they won't suffer much shock from being transplanted, as they haven't been traumatically dug up. Usually, container-grown trees are rootbound (meaning the roots don't have anywhere to go, so they get tangled up inside the pot). To fix this, make a few slices through a root wad, like cutting a wedding cake.

Bareroot trees

have been dug up and stored without any soil. This makes them cheap to dig, store, and ship; therefore, they're cheaper for you to buy. They're easy to plant, although you can set them in only at certain times of the year (spring is best, before they break bud), and not every kind of tree is available in this manner.

Wanna learn how to plant these puppies? Turn to Plant It Like You Mean It (page 78). All done now? Spend some time coloring the gnome on page 68.

Color me Gnome

1 = Mandevilla pink

2 = Calamondin orange

3 = Crimson rose

6 = Black mondo

5 = Fern green   7 = Alyssum white

6 = Petunia purple

COMPOSTEST IS THE MOSTEST

Composting is all about the circle of life, my friend.

In composting, leftovers become fertilizer for your vegetable garden (page 75) so you can grow more food. Your weeds transform themselves into the perfect soil when sandwiched between layers of crap soil that you've dug out and old leaves and grass clippings.

Some people will tell you that composting is a science, but I can TESTIFY that it's a no-brainer.

The most that's required is that you throw stuff in a pile in a somewhat sunny spot. Then wait a few months, and you'll be feasting on the resulting awesomeness.

To get your doctorate, though, buy or construct fancy bins or barrels and then carefully select waste materials to put in them in a layered fashion. Eventually, sift the results. When whatever you've composted has broken down to the point that it looks like loose, crumbly soil, you won. Use and enjoy!

You can compost: garden trimmings, old soil, vegetable and fruit scraps, eggs and cardboard egg cartons, orange peels, the contents of the vacuum bag, coffee grounds, seaweed, weeds (lay them in the driveway for a few days to be sure they're dead; you don't want fertile ground for the seeds), old bouquets, leftover bread.

I don't have an issue with critters getting into my business, but maybe you do. If that's the case, get a bin with a lid that fits securely. Also, keep animal products like cheese and bones out of the pile to make it less appealing to wildlife.

I have composted in lovingly made wood and wire bins, a store-bought barrel, chicken-wire tubes, an old kick drum, a plain ol' pile, and some admittedly bizarre experiments. They all worked. Stuff rots. It's nature's way.

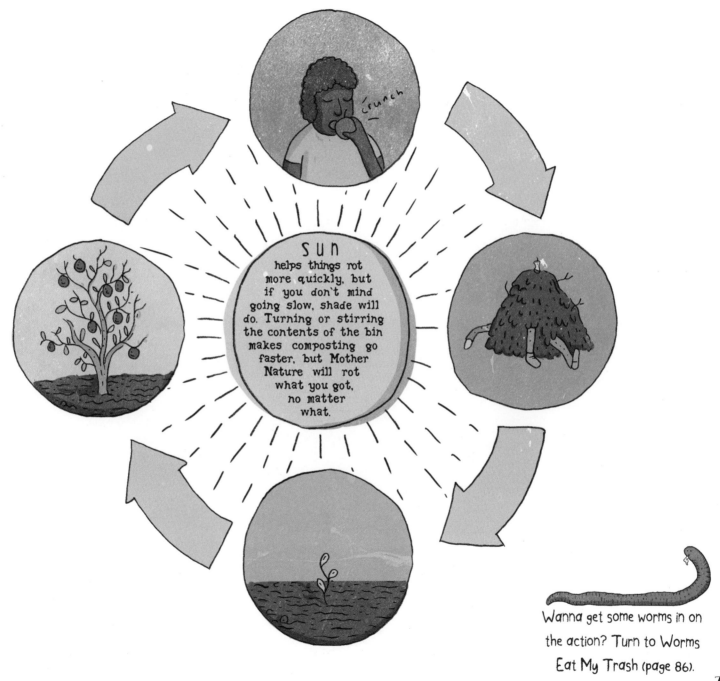

SUN helps things rot more quickly, but if you don't mind going slow, shade will do. Turning or stirring the contents of the bin makes composting go faster, but Mother Nature will rot what you got, no matter what.

crunch

Wanna get some worms in on the action? Turn to Worms Eat My Trash (page 86).

Sandy Handy...

I've had loose, sandy soil. It was amazing:

I could grow plants I never dreamed of because of the fantastic drainage. Lots of plants demand good drainage. I couldn't keep anything wet for even a minute, however, so everything that likes water hated me. Also, it was tricky keeping things fertilized. The soil (and I) had a parched look all the time.

To amend sandy soil, start by looking at yourself in the mirror long and hard. Do you really deserve better? Yes? Then think about adding mushroom compost or sphagnum moss.

If you live close to a beach or desert, make sure you're working with plants that are in harmony with your environment, even though that can put a crimp in your options. For example? Don't try to plant a lush green lawn in the desert, and don't plant a vegetable garden at the beach. Go for dune grasses at the beach and cacti in the desert. This simple logic will save you a ton of scratch, which will make you feel better about your limited choices.

I'm stoked to tell you that I'm going to talk to you about composting on page 70. Composting is the way to go. Once you do it, you get sort of cultlike about it.
Kinda like people who do yoga.

Believe it or not, just as we do, roots need air to survive and thrive. Think about it: Roots don't grow in the soil — they grow in the spaces *between* the particles. Wait, did I just BLOW YOUR MIND?

You might be thinking about dumping peat into your sandy soil to make it absorb more water. Think twice, yo. Peat is cool, but earth-lovers don't go for it, because after it's been mined, the bogs it came from take hundreds of years to re-form. Besides, you're robbing the world of precious future coal and diamonds. **YOU'RE NOT WORTH IT, DUDE.**

Tree to be you & me

From a towering oak to a dwarf flowering almond, let me help you decide what to put where. There are few things in life I'll splurge on (pretty much paint and trees; you don't want to cheap out on either), but trees are worth the cash outlay. The Lorax was right. Trees are the best! They provide shade, habitat for birds, and legitimacy. Lovely fall color, privacy from neighbors, apples and pears... heck! Maple syrup!

At the same time, trees are BIG and permanent, so plant them the right way. You don't want a poorly situated tree to fall on the house during a storm or have a tree that grows so big that it tangles with power lines or ruins your cable reception. Expensive to buy and labor-intensive to plant, I'm telling you, trees can be difficult. The best things in the garden usually involve the most work, though, eh?

A tree is more of a commitment than buying a parrot or, say, getting married is. Think it through before you remove a tree that could be a century old and before you plant a tree that could get so enormous that it threatens the neighborhood.

You may want to consult a pro on this one, bro. Flip to One, Two, Tree (page 52).

Learn about really big trees on page 80 and about medium-sized trees on page 88.

If you give up and default to build a treeless 'scape, turn to Shrubs: The Khaki Pants of the Landscape (page 79).

HELP! I NEED SOMEBODY

Aside from the kinds of help I've already mentioned (and I've mentioned a lot, if I do say so myself), there are professional gardeners and garden coaches.

TIME TO PRUNE THE BUDDLEIA!

Professional gardener

This person knows her stuff, plant-wise. She's usually a horticulturist, which is Latin "knows when to prune the buddleia." You can hire a gardener to deadhead, divide plants, and generally know what to do and when to do it. She'll tell you the names of things you didn't know weren't weeds. She'll know how to make things grow. Usually, a quick stop from a gardener every couple of weeks is enough to keep you looking pretty for not a lot of dough. Look for a Master Gardener group and ask around for two or three who will hire themselves out. Talk to a few, and compare hourly rates.

Garden coach

This person is just like a professional gardener, in that he knows his stuff, but he won't want to lift a finger. He's who you want if you actually want to learn how to garden for yourself. He'll teach you. A garden coach is also a go-to for recommendations on every garden-related job you need done. Want to know which company to call to do what you don't want to do (like mowing the lawn)? A garden coach will point you in the right direction. He'll be filled with ideas and usually has so much knowledge crammed in his cranium that it's amazing his head doesn't blow up.

If you have a very small design project, a gardener or garden coach will be able to help you way more inexpensively than a landscape architect or a garden designer will. For anything bigger than very small, see what a coach or gardener is willing to take on.

Ready to get it done? Flip to Rip It Up (page 56) or go back to designing it yourself at Landstalking™ (page 16).

 EAT IT

I strongly suggest you designate a space for growing your own vegetables and maybe even some fruit. It's more satisfying than you could imagine, and easy, too!

The first thing veggies need is a sunny spot (8 hours of sun) with a hose hookup nearby. The area should have good soil: Test it, yo (see Soil, Yourself, page 62). If you think your soil is dodgy, consider a raised bed filled with compost and other good stuff.

Figure out how much space you can assign to a vegetable garden before you think about what to grow. A small, 4-by-4-foot plot is enough room for a tomato plant, some lettuce, and a few herbs. Don't venture into cucumbers, squash, more than one tomato, or any corn at all unless you have a large space, because these things get BIG.

Start small, you can always make it bigger next year.

Pick a site near the house, so harvesting doesn't become a schlep-fest, okay?

You can make a good raised bed from a simple wooden frame. Use cedar: It's slow to rot and it's not full o' chemicals. Or build it with any kind of untreated lumber, but plan on replacing it when it rots. See if I care. Then fill it with the good stuff (turn to Compostest Is the Mostest, page 70).

Learn more about what you can grow at Grow What? (page 108). Or discover interesting stuff about herbs by turning to Herbie, Fully Loaded (page 110).

There are "patio-size" tomato plants, cucumbers, and strawberries, for example, on the way from a plant breeder near you. Good for small gardens and containers!

Reasons to Grow

1. To survive the Apocalypse

2. To be smugger than all the other people who can "hear the sustainability."

3. It beats watching reality television

4. You've never truly sweated until you can tomatoes in the middle of August.

5. Real strawberries = real tears of joy.

6. Garlic and garlic chives repel vampires

your own Food

 7. You can't go to the grocery store naked . . . again.

 10. You won't hug a stranger, but you'll eat that head of lettuce from Peru?

 8. You can pretend to "talk to the camera" like you're the host of a gardening show.

 11. You've secretly always wanted to be a hippie.

 9. A sun-warmed tomato brings you close to God (or Dog, if you're dyslexic).

 12. You like the idea of purple carrots, yellow cucumbers, and pink potatoes.

PLANT IT LIKE YOU MEAN IT

If you buy a B&B tree or shrub, treat that root ball as if it was a precious baby made out of glass and porcelain. You hear me?

The hole you dig for it should be as deep as the root ball actually is but twice as wide. Get that root ball in the hole, gently. The tree should ultimately rest so that the root flare is at ground level. Makes sense, right? Cut the ropes that hold the burlap and peel off all the malarkey that's holding everything together. Now backfill the soil around the tree. Mix a nice little cocktail of the original soil, compost, and some composted manure for a happier tree. Last, form a little pool around the base of the trunk to hold water. While it's new,

all its roots are concentrated right there, so might as well have the water stay there. Then water well.

A shrub or tree grown in a container is the easiest to plant — just dig a hole, lay the plant on its side so you can slide off the pot, pop the plant into the hole, and backfill. Use the soil cocktail and the little pool I mentioned above, and voilà!

Usually, you order bareroot plants through the mail. The second they arrive, you've got to get those roots in water. Let them soak it up! (Just overnight, though.) Prune away any parts damaged in shipping. Dig a hole big enough to spread out those roots. Make a cone in the middle to help figure out what

height the tree should be at and to give you something to spread the roots over. Then backfill, using that same soil cocktail.

Now, because this tree has nothing to anchor it down, I insist you stake it. Insert two stakes on opposite sides of the tree. Tie them to the tree using wire that you've slid through small pieces of old garden hose. (This trick is so the wire doesn't cut into the tree.)

You've got to check the tree's stability every once in a while by giving it a little shake. Remove the stakes as soon as the tree is able to stand on its own two feet or it will never get strong on its own.

You're done! Now you can color the gnome on page 68.

SHRUBS: THE KHAKI PANTS OF THE LANDSCAPE

Shrubs are the Rodney Dangerfields of the home landscape. They don't get any respect. Does that reference date me? Probably.

Shrubs make it all work and yet, because they're almost no fun to buy, they totally get shafted all the time. Flowers are sexy, trees give you shade or fruit, vegetables are all tasty and good for you, and shrubs, well . . .

But here's the deal. There are some mega rad shrubs out there, stuff you can almost get excited about. You can get flowers out of them, some even bear fruit! Some are pretty in winter, some look good all year. These are plants that work for you, and they make other things work better.

Hydrangea This is a shrub! Half the population flips over it and the other 50 percent has no clue what it is. But if they did? They'd probably flip too.

Hydrangea • *Hydrangea* species

Blueberry If I told you there was a beautiful shrub that sports lovely little white bell flowers in spring and has damn sexy, blazing fall color and even has blueberries on it, would you believe me?

Blueberry • *Vaccinium* species

Redtwig dogwood Those pretty red twigs you see in containers in winter? They're even prettier in your yard. And easy to deal with 365.

Redtwig dogwood • *Cornus sericea*

Boxwood Boxwood hedges. Sigh. You probably want some separating you from the neighbors. Try Hedge Fun(d) (page 57).

Boxwood • *Buxus* species

I admit it: I need more shrubbery. My yard lacks structure and I know it. If your yard has lots of plants in it but looks disorganized, that's probably your prob, too.

If you don't want to flip to Flowering Shrubs (page 96) to learn more, there's something wrong with you. This topic is fascinating.

BIG, BIG TREES

A big tree makes me nervous. Maybe you should skip it and put in a big patio umbrella instead.

Anyway, let's use an oak as an example. Say you want to buy an oak. Okay, someone 10 years ago had to plant a zillion acorns to get you that tree. For 10 years people cared for that tree, watered it, and fed it. Then someone came and dug it up, either by hand (preferred but adds to price) or with a tree spade attached to a truck. Then that root ball was wrapped in burlap and watered, and then watched to make sure it handled the digging. Eventually it makes it to you. This tree starts at 60 feet and reaches to the moon. How do you put a price tag on that?

Oak. It starts with an acorn and can live hundreds of years and get quite, quite big. Talk about commitment. If you plant one, get ready for squirrels, because they'll be relentless in fall when the acorns come.

Sycamore. This tree is easy to identify because the trunk looks like it could use a good exfoliation. It can get to over 100 feet and the leaves are gigantic. Keep in mind that come autumn, you will need a GIANT rake for those GIANT leaves.

Bald cypress. This tree has needles but isn't evergreen. It's like a leather jacket over a lace dress: rough and tough bark with delicate, ferny foliage. It will tolerate wet spots and gets taller than Paul Bunyan.

Ginkgo.
Like dinosaurs? Dinosaurs liked the ginkgo, until they died. This tree has cool, Shrek-colored leaves that turn brilliant yellow in fall. There are males and females; be sure to buy yourself a male, as the fruit that falls from the female smells like someone yakked all over your yard. A ginkgo makes a great "street tree."

Maple.
The maple is all about two things: fall color and maple syrup. Norway maples are considered invasive in some areas. Sugar maples are pretty and you can legitimately get syrup from them, if you have a month to collect and boil down the sap.

Always buy the biggest, oldest tree you can afford. Always. I'm cheap, cheaper than you are, but I know to go spendy on big trees.

Daunted and thinking smaller? Try Happy Medium Trees (page 88). A lot smaller? Go to Shrubs: The Khaki Pants of the Landscape (page 79). Master those and you can work your way up!

Oak = *Quercus* species. Sycamore = *Platanus occidentalis*. Bald cypress = *Taxodium dystichum*. Gingko = *Gingko biloba*. Maple = *Acer* species. Norway maple = *Acer platanoides*. Sugar maple = *Acer saccharum*

Design Hints

Setting up your perennial garden may seem intimidating, but don't be afraid. Perennials are just plants. And truly, if one or nine don't work out, you can dig them up and move them to a new spot ... like 18 times.

When I'm making a garden, I set the plants, in their pots, exactly where I'm thinking of planting them, stand back, rearrange, rearrange some more, then leave them until I'm sure I have just the right look. A boring and perhaps geriatric gardener would tell you to put the tall stuff in back and work forward to the short stuff. Occasionally, I like to shake things up and put a grouping of the same tall plants someplace in the middle of things. I'm an anarchist.

I like to use a variety of foliage textures, too. Try putting a plant with large chunky leaves next to one with ferny leaves and maybe another with strappy leaves (like an iris). I also love plants whose leaves aren't green. I think they make the whole thing look a little more ... spectacular!*

When you're satisfied, plant 'em, water 'em, and stand back and admire 'em. Then pat yourself on the back.

Traditionally, BIG backyards mean BIG plants. Look at giant grasses and plants that multiply quickly, and make sure to use huge quantities of each plant you choose. Your aim is to have the overall look be bold and in scale, not like the view from an airplane at 5,000 feet.

Be sure you know the plants' ultimate height and spread before you dig, then plant them accordingly. It may — will — should — look sparse, but you'll thank me later.

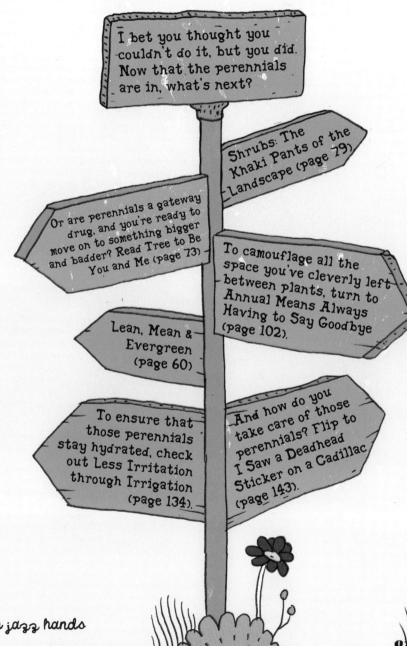

I bet you thought you couldn't do it, but you did. Now that the perennials are in, what's next?

Shrubs: The Khaki Pants of the Landscape (page 79)

Or are perennials a gateway drug, and you're ready to move on to something bigger and badder? Read Tree to Be You and Me (page 73)

To camouflage all the space you've cleverly left between plants, turn to Annual Means Always Having to Say Goodbye (page 102).

Lean, Mean & Evergreen (page 60)

To ensure that those perennials stay hydrated, check out Less Irritation through Irrigation (page 134).

And how do you take care of those perennials? Flip to I Saw a Deadhead Sticker on a Cadillac (page 143).

*Said with jazz hands

Worms Eat My Trash

You can compost by letting worms eat your garbage. I'm serious.

You can buy or make a worm bin (mine is purchased and I'll tell you why in a minute) that becomes habitat for thousands of worms, then you feed them your leftovers, paper, eggshells, cardboard, coffee filters, tea bags, corncobs, and onion skins. Just skip meat, dairy, and anything oily or greasy.

Most worm bins have three trays, each with a perforated bottom so the worms can get around. In the bottom tray, you set up a nice little nest for them with shredded coconut husks (or shredded newspaper) and then you tuck food down in that stuff for them. Once the worm population gets established, you can pile food in the upper trays, too. You'll be amazed at how fast they cruise right through it, transforming it into luscious castings. It takes a few months to establish a worm bin, but you'll be glad to have it!

Now, the benefits are that you're not sending trash to the landfill *and* you get to add worm poop to your garden. The little guys' poop is the world's best fertilizer. And then there's this liquid that accumulates from the rotting food that drips through all the poop and gathers at the bottom of the bin. It's not pretty, but it's SUPER GARDEN SAUCE.

A store-bought worm bin comes with a spigot at the bottom, which will assist you in collecting this SUPER GARDEN SAUCE. See, this is why mine is purchased.

SUPER GARDEN SAUCE is so great that I give it as a gift, but only to those in the know. It's free for me and a priceless fertilizer for them.

The kind of worms you need are called red wrigglers. Order them off the Internet and then you'll come home from work someday to a box of worms on your doorstep, on purpose.

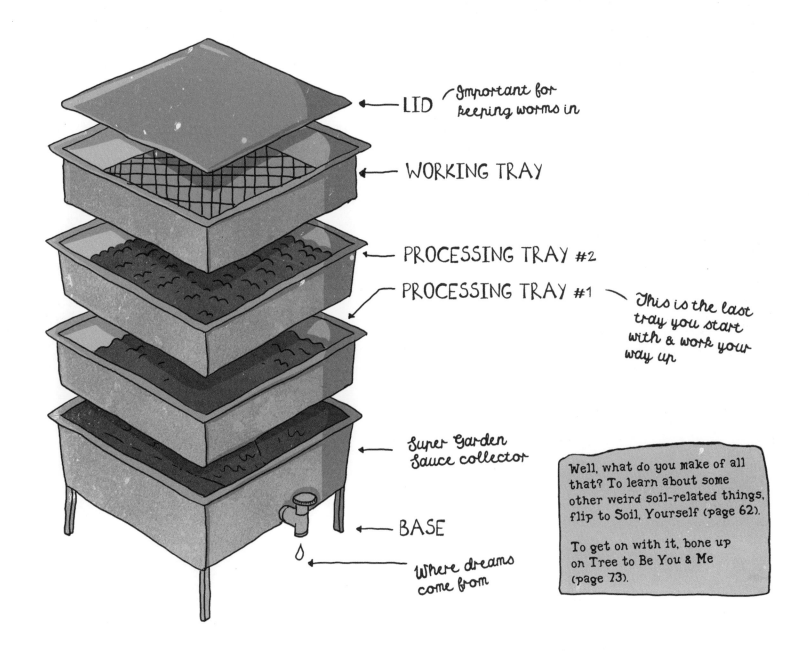

LID — *Important for keeping worms in*

WORKING TRAY

PROCESSING TRAY #2

PROCESSING TRAY #1 — *This is the last tray you start with & work your way up*

Super Garden Sauce collector

BASE

Where dreams come from

Well, what do you make of all that? To learn about some other weird soil-related things, flip to Soil, Yourself (page 62).

To get on with it, bone up on Tree to Be You & Me (page 73).

Happy Medium Trees

I feel so much safer talking to you about medium-size trees. These are trees that can't hurt you, and some of them even flower. Everyone wins.

These trees range from 30 to 60 feet tall. Circle the ones that sound good to you.

Crab Apple

Callery Pear

Apple and crab apple.

Apples and crab apples are sisters, but one sister is easier to get along with than the other. (Isn't that always the way it is?) Both produce beautiful flowers in late spring, and then all hell breaks loose. They're susceptible to mildew, apple scab (less pleasant than it sounds), fire blight (as bad as it sounds), and aphids (see page 152), but a lot of breeding has been done to bring a new generation of arse-whoopin' crab apples that say "Bring. It. On." Try *Malus sargentii* 'Adirondack' or 'PrairieFire'. Apples are a lot fussier, in many ways, but the cruddiest part is that they must be sprayed with awful chemicals for the fruits to look like you're used to seeing them. If you don't spray, they'll get attacked by one insect after another, and you'll have fruit all over the ground, fermenting and stinking up the place. And setting the table for drunk, angry hornets. Stick with non-edible crab apple, spectacular in spring.

Callery pear.
You'll find this a lot in cities. It's super-resistant to pretty much everything. Its tall, narrow form complements tall, narrow buildings. The flowers, however, have a particular stink to them. Also, some cultivars are weak in wind or snow, so make sure you're getting a new and improved strain like 'Autumn Blaze' or 'Aristocrat'.

Red Horse Chestnut

White Birch

Mulberry

Red horse chestnut.
This really cute tree bears giant, gorgeous clusters of red flowers. You should get one.

White birch.
Everyone loves that flaky white bark, including moose (and birch borers). So if you have a moose allergy, think twice about planting one.

Mulberry.
It's cheap, fast-growing, and short-lived. And the fruit tastes bad. So if you don't want birds pooping mulberries all over your car, skip this one.

Fast-growing trees are cheap.
That said, they may not be the easiest things to maintain. Some require a lot of pruning to keep them looking the way you want. Also, they may not have the strongest support system, since they grew so dang fast, and they'll be weak and brittle.

Want something smaller? Flip to Wee Trees (page 98). Or shake it up and look at, say, ground covers, Go to LawnTurnatives™ (page 132).

Everyone knows that a crab apple derives its name from the taste of its fruit, which is distinctively crustacean. Ahem.

Apple and crab apple = *Malus* species.
Callery pear = *Pyrus calleryana*.
Mulberry = *Morus* species.
Red horse chestnut = *Aesculus x carnea*.
White birch = *Betula papyrifera*.

LANDSCAPING MAD LIBS

With a partner, choose a word for each number.
Then have your buddy plug your words
into the sentences on the next page and let the
landscape hilarity ensue!

1 _____
   Adjective

2 _____
   Scary plural noun

3 _____
   Plural noun

4 _____
   Adjective

5 _____
   A friend's name

6 _____
   Plural noun

7 _____
   Plural noun

8 _____
   Noun

9 _____
   Verb ending in "ing"

My front yard looks

_____ because of
       1

_____ and _____ . I
    2   3

wish it was more _____ .
                     4

I wish my yard looked more

like _____'s. He/she has
         5

lots of _____ and _____
           6   7

I'm envious of.

Holy _____ ! My backyard
         8

needs some serious _____ !
                        9

Kinda Shady

If I had a shade/
part-shade garden, and I do,
the first thing I'd think of is to
thin out the trees above it to let in
as much light as possible (see
One, Two, Tree, page 52, about
hiring a tree guy to do this).
Because shade can be rough, yo.

The problem with a shade garden is
that people want the colors of
a sun garden in a shady spot. And
it just isn't possible. There are
GORGEOUS plants for shade
out there, but they're more about
leaves and textures than about
flowers and colors.

Let's meet the shade plants:

Astilbe
This showy plant,
with its fernlike leaves,
sports feathers
of red, pink, purple,
or white flowers in
summer.

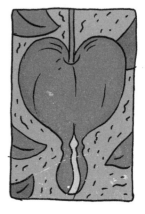

Bleeding heart
A tall, graceful spring
bloomer, bleeding
heart, in pink or white,
dies to the ground in
the heat of summer.

Some shade plants need a bit more moisture.
If you have dry shade (and that's typical), go to
Less Irritation through Irrigation (page 134).

Or get your bad self the heck out of here and read all
about ground covers in LawnTurnatives™ (page 132).

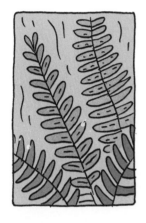

Ferns

There are zillions, in all heights. Some — the Japanese painted fern, for example — present interesting colors.

Hosta

With this plant, it's all about the leaves: colored, variegated, puckered, you name it. There are almost countless varieties. They flower, but that's not the allure. Hostas are great for dry shade.

Hakone grass

This groovy little floppy grass comes in an array of colors that light up a dark spot.

Goatsbeard

It's as if a cream astilbe and Godzilla had a love child.

Astilbe = *Astilbe* species. Bleeding heart = *Dicentra* species. Ferns = *Dryopteris, Athyrium,* and other species. Goatsbeard = *Aruncus* species. Hakone grass = *Hakonechloa* species. Hosta = *Hosta* species

YOUR A** IS GRASS

Those big ol' perennial grasses we all admire require little care, but that care is different from what other kinds of plants (called "broadleaf") need. For example, killing a grass by over- or underwatering is pretty rare after the first year of acclimating. Its roots stretch down as far as the grass grows tall, and just as wide, which helps to protect it from all sorts of malarkey, like prairie fires, drought, and erosion.

The downside is that those same roots make a grass mega challenging to move, so before you put plant to soil, double- and triple-check how big that bad boy will get because — no kidding — I've had to use an ax to get a grass out of the ground.

Here are a few grasses I'd like you to meet:

Blue fescue This is short and a chalky blue when planted in full sun; it's brown and dead in the shade.

Carex Short and moppy, carex is fun in sun or a gay blade in the shade, and sometimes evergreen.

Feather reed grass This grass has a good posture in full sun, not as slouchy as some others. It reaches to 4 feet tall and blooms in summer

Fountain grass This belongs to the "cute family" of grasses. It's relatively small, less than 4 feet tall at maturity, and cascades (hence the name). All members of the family have fluffy "flowers."

Another weird thing about grasses? You leave the dead blades and spent blooms throughout winter (adding interest to the landscape when there's almost nothing else) and then cut them down in spring. I like to bungee them up like a ponytail and then cut about 4 inches from the bottom in late March. They start growing again shortly after that.

Grasses are super for absorbing sound. Is everyone in your household a screamer? Plant a few dozen . . .

How can you show them off? Check out Design Hints (page 82).

How about some vines? Turn to Antisocial Climbers (page 106).

Design Hints (page 82).

How about some vines? Turn to Antisocial Climbers (page 106).

Blue fescue = *Festuca glauca*

Carex = *Carex* species

Feather reed grass = *Calamagrostis* species

Fountain grass = *Pennisetum* species

Japanese blood grass = *Imperata cylindrica* 'Red Baron'

Miscanthus = *Miscanthus* species

Northern sea oat = *Chasmanthium latifolium*

Switchgrass = *Panicum* species

Japanese blood grass Pretty straight blades of grass are tipped with blood red. Each is about 12 inches tall. This grass doesn't clump; it's a runner. It will weave around other plants and become a great ground cover.

Miscanthus The Bad Boy of grasses, all of its brothers are BIG, and the granddaddy of them all, *Miscanthus sinensis*, is invasive in some states. For whatever reason, the cool, stripy ones aren't quite as rampant; if you select one of those, you're golden.

Northern sea oat This is, well, oaty-looking. It grows to 3 feet tall, sort of bamboolike. Its seeds show up everywhere, which I enjoy, plus it can take some shade.

Switchgrass Taller and lacier than Mr. Miscanthus, switchgrass shows excellent fall color.

flowering Shrubs

They start in spring with forsythias, azaleas, and rhododendrons. And then you have the hydrangeas, weigelas, and ... hey, did you know that some roses are considered shrubs? Here's a brief rundown, kind of in order of bloom.

Butterfly bush.

This is a subshrub in colder climates, which means it dies to the ground in winter, where you have winter, and it races back to shrub-sized again in summer. That means you actually cut it back in spring and let it grow, fresh, each year. As its name implies (shouts), this is a butterfly magnet, and it smells good enough to be a people magnet. You should find a place for it, if you live where it isn't invasive. And where that's a problem, consider moving to where it isn't, because it's awesome.

Hydrangea.

There are, technically, many kinds of hydrangea. I want you to pay attention to two kinds: the pains in the ass and the easy-peasy ones. If you want the big, floppy blue or pink cauliflower-head-style ones, you're in for a world of hurt. In cold climates they don't flower at all, and they never turn out the right color in any climate. Just skip it, man. On the flip side, hydrangeas like the oak-leaf variety and 'Limelight' are a joy to have around and will give you as much trouble as a pet rock.

Forsythia.

Meh. I like them in my neighbor's yard for the three weeks they're flowering, but for the rest of the year, there is NOTHING special about them.

Butterfly bush = *Buddleia* species. Hydrangea = *Hydrangea* species. Oakleaf hydrangea = *Hydrangea quercifolia*. 'Limelight' hydrangea = *Hydrangea paniculata* 'Limelight', lilac = *Syringa* species. Forsythia = *Forsythia* species. Viburnum = *Viburnum* species. Azalea and rhododendron = *Rhododendron* species. Ninebark = *Physocarpus opulifolius*. Shrub rose = *Rosa* species. Spirea = *Spiraea* species. Weigela = *Weigela* species. Yucca = *Yucca* species.

Viburnum.

There are quite a few kinds of viburnum. Some smell like a dream when in bloom, and though I can't say that any of them is Miss Ornamental Shrub 2017, I've never been let down.

Azalea and rhododendron.

Without acidic soil (see Dropping Acid, page 54), you'll probably fail with either of these (they're in the same family). Oh, but you say you do have acidic soil? Holy bold spring color, Batman! And it's evergreen, too!

Ninebark.

So dramatic, I think it's good enough to be at least a twelvebark. My favorite has weirdly chocolate brown leaves, grows like it has someplace to be later, and is highly tolerant of drought.

Shrub rose.

There are tons of super-flowering, low-maintenance shrub roses out there, like the Knockouts and the Meidiland series. These require no extra care: Just plant them, and remove any dead twigs in spring.

Spirea.

Please, skip this plant. It's boring and overused. And where it's overused, it's usually also badly cared for. Just skip it.

Weigela.

Wonky-shaped and uneven, tropical-looking weigela comes with variegated leaves or all sorts of browns and coppers. It has bold flowers in early summer and often repeat-blooms later. I think you need some.

Yucca.

Not very shrubby, really. Its long, needlelike, and strappy leaves come in a few colors, striped and solid. It throws out a tall tower of bell-shaped flowers and it's evergreen. What's not to like?

Check out Lean, Mean & Evergreen (Page 60). ★ Or live dangerously and learn all about hedges at Hedge Fun(d) (Page 57).

Wee Trees

Ooooh, I'm in my happy place.

These trees are considered ornamentals or even understory trees. What does all that mean? Maybe these trees do nothing but be pretty to look at. Or some of them started out as trees that grew under bigger trees. As a city girl, I see lots of these trees, and for good reason. They're steady, sturdy, and attractive, and they all grow to be shorter than 30 feet tall.

Dogwood.

Pagoda or kousa, this is a simple, pleasant, medium-size flowering tree. The kousa has a straight trunk, laughs at plagues and agues, has four-petaled white flowers in late spring, and sports red leaves in fall. The pagoda is a slower grower with lacy flowers, and also has colorful foliage in late fall; its leaves turn an awesome burgundy. It also boasts blackish-blue berries.

Japanese maple.

There are so many kinds that they're collectible. Some are upright, others are weeping; some are red, some are green; and there's every combination of mash-up. Some are green weepers, some are red and upright. Some are green and upright, some are red weepers that wish they were upright. Some wear funny hats. They appear delicate, but they're tougher than Mr. T before he's had his morning coffee. I think you need one. Or six.

Japanese tree lilac.

Its claim to fame is fragrant, giant panicles of white flowers in early summer. Otherwise, it's unremarkable: It provides no cool fall color, berries, rad bark, or show tunes. But oh, the fragrance . . .

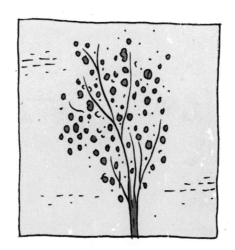

Redbud.

Dang, I love this tree. Heart-shaped leaves follow the late-spring show — branches that flower right out of the bark. It looks as if someone has strung pink twinkle lights throughout the branches. There's a purple-leaved variety called 'Forest Pansy' that could be called 'Hot Pants', as far as I'm concerned.

Serviceberry.

This tree is near perfect: sweet white flowers in spring, delicious berries in summer, and awesome autumn color. Also, when the berries get old and frazzled, they ferment, and birds that eat them get tipsy and act goofy. Do it.

Star magnolia.

Early blooms blow off in blustery spring weather, but this wee tree is slow-growing with showy, Mae West white or pink flowers, and they make this wee tree worth the space it takes up.

Scared? It's okay to skip over to Hire a Guy (page 22) to find out how to get help with some of the bigger trees.

If you think you can do it, check out the shrubs on page 79 so that your new tree friends won't be lonely.

I bet you'd also get a kick out of Still Life with Mulch (page 125).

Pagoda dogwood = *Cornus alternifolia*
Kousa dogwood = *Cornus kousa*
Japanese maple = *Acer palmatum*
Japanese tree lilac = *Syringa reticulata*
Redbud = *Cercis canadensis*
Serviceberry = *Amelanchier* species
Star magnolia = *Magnolia stellata*

SUNNY DAY REAL ESTATE

Sunny perennials are a joy to buy, plant, and watch as they grow. It's a simple, straightforward situation, and it comes down to picking plants that appeal to you and layering them just right. Kind of like getting dressed in the morning.

So, pick out stuff you like. Read the tags or ask someone how tall they get, when they flower, and whether they need any special handling. Then go ahead: Plant masses of them!

The following plants are as steady as a seventh-grade boyfriend:

Daylily.
There are scads of cultivars. They bloom in summer; some repeat, but weakly. They come in all colors and sizes.

Black-eyed Susan.
This one blooms from late summer into fall; to 24 inches.

Aster.
Fall blooming, some need pinching so as not to look like a hobo.

Daisy.
This will be 24–36 inches of happy flowers for most of the summer, especially with deadheading.

Coneflower.
With faithful deadheading, you get flowers for most of the summer and into fall; 24 inches.

Dianthus.
No one wants a bouquet of carnations (one kind of dianthis), but the carnation's short, clove-scented cousins (called pinks) are pretty cool.

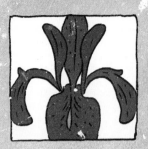

Iris.
With the gazillion choices, something will fit your conditions. Some like it hot and dry, some dig water, they all crave sun. Bloom is in late spring.

Peony.
Green and shrubby, this plant needs a cage to hold it up. It sports showy flowers, but they're a mess after a heavy downpour. So what? Pray for sunny days and enjoy.

Phlox.
Panicles of flowers in a wide range of colors bloom from mid- to late summer. Consider phlox a requirement.

Poppy.
This perennial will pop up in spring, bloom in late spring, then wither away and seem to die in midsummer. Not so: It'll be back next spring.

Lavender.
Leaves and flowers smell heavenly. It requires hot and dry, and won't do well in loam.

The rule is to set out plants in groups of three or five or even seven, if you have a large space. Odd numbers are supposed to look more natural. I think that's crap. There are a lot of plants out there that are special enough that you only need one (called a specimen plant). You *do* want to be careful not to have too many onesies in your garden, though — that would look like a freak show. Do try to have groupings of the same plant and do show off the wonders of a really special plant.

Don't buy plants that are all flowering at the same time. You want to stagger blooms to get color all summer long, right?

Got shade? Flip to Kinda Shady (page 92). Want to know about designing with perennials? Consult Forever Yours, Perennials (page 119).

Aster = *Aster* species. Black-eyed Susan = *Rudbeckia* species. Coneflower = *Echinacea* species. Daisy = *Leucanthemum* species. Daylily = *Hemerocallis* species. Dianthus = *Dianthus* species. Iris = *Iris* species. Lavender = *Lavandula* species. Peony = *Paeonia* species. Phlox = *Phlox* species. Poppy = *Papaver* species

Annual Means Always

Annuals bring on the flash. They don't stop blooming until it gets cold, then they die. Plant them in containers or in beds and let them do their thing. I'm a big fan. Here are some annuals you probably already know:

Alyssum

In white or pastel colors, alyssum hugs the ground with bazillions of tiny flowers and a sweet smell you either love or hate.

Begonia

Members of this family are great for shade, and some new varieties are HUGE.

Dusty miller

Harmless silver (almost white) foliage.

Fuchsia

Shaped like a Victorian dress, wacky-colored fuchsia is great for shade, part shade, or a hanging basket.

Having To Say Goodbye

Calibrachoa

This looks like a petunia but is way hipper. It'll trail over the side of a pot or hug the ground.

Coleus

This plant sports multicolored foliage galore, more vibrant in shade. You'll love it.

Geranium

You know this plant well (except for its real name, maybe : pelargonium). Everyone grows it, so I don't want to encourage it.

Impatiens

So boring, so overused . . . and yet, so useful. One flat and you've got a ton of flowers. Impatiens does fine in sun, but you'll get better color in shade.

Annual Means Always

Dahlia

If you've got a spot with full sun, dahlia is a must. Trust me.

Marigold

Remember sprouting seeds in a Dixie cup in second grade? Probably marigold. This tough plant lasts into fall.

When planting in beds, consider the mature height and spread of each annual (or perennial, for that matter) and design accordingly. Putting them in pots? Pack 'em in, yo.

Lantana

Weird flowers radiate hot colors like laser beams. This plant likes it hot and dry.

Petunia

This old-fashioned plant is becoming popular again, thanks to cracked-out varieties that grow like crayzay.

Having To Say Goodbye

PART DEUX

Purple Heart

This easy plant, sometimes called a wandering Jew (really), thrives in full sun or no sun. No water? That's fine too. Purple flowers complement purple leaves.

Salvia

This is a mostly red or blue, tall and narrow annual that butterflies and hummingbirds flock to.

Canna

At 2 to 6 feet tall, this statuesque tropical often has colored foliage, and the flowers are as loud as trumpets when they get going.

Easy-peasy. What's next?

Learn about watering at Less Irritation through Irrigation (page 134).

Got a problem? Consult Weeds Happen (page 154).

To expand your garden, go to Decks in the City (page 49).

Antisocial Climbers

Vines are great for bringing interest to vertical surfaces, like walls, trellises, and things that are ugly and too heavy to move. There are perennial vines and annual vines. With perennial vines, there are grabbers and stickers.

Sort of like dating . . .

The grabbers shoot up fast and wrap themselves around a trellis and branches, always moving up and out. The stickers take things slow, making their own adhesive that enables them to stick to surfaces that don't have things for them to grab on to. Among grabbers are clematis, honeysuckle, hops, and wisteria. Some stickers are Boston ivy, climbing hydrangea, English ivy, and Virginia creeper.

Grabbers

Clematis. I love the flowers, which come in lots of colors and shapes. For thick foliage cover, though, look someplace else. Clematis vines put their time and energy into remarkable blooms and not in making zillions of leaves.

Honeysuckle. Honeysuckle flirts with hummingbirds and bees, and scrambles over whatever it can.

Hops. Hops put forth great growth, perfect for covering a fence or a trellis. Sure, the flowers aren't showy, but you can make beer out of them. A decent trade-off, yes?

Wisteria. When I worked in a garden center and someone asked whether she should buy a wisteria, I'd say, "Would you recommend having a second husband?" Because it's *that* much work. With its staggering rate of growth, it'll take over like Godzilla, so be prepared to do major pruning to keep it off the neighbor's roof.

HONEYSUCKLE

Stickers

Boston ivy and Virginia creeper. These cousins are hardcore (like, growing up to 50 feet in length). They'll climb on anything, so be sure to pull the car into the garage at night.

Climbing hydrangea. This is great for a shady spot, and is an easygoing vine. It's also slow growing; be sure to prune it only right after it's finished flowering.

English ivy. Slow growing and stringy, English ivy is cool because it's evergreen. Here in Chicago, we coax it to grow over many, many years. In other parts of the country, it's completely invasive. So know your ivy!

· CLEMATIS ·

WISTERIA

Show-Offs!

Annual vines

These are a lot showier than any perennial vines. They're pretty much all grabbers.

Hyacinth bean. This fast-growing, purple vine is covered with cute lavender flowers and long, purple, edible beans.

Mandevilla. This tropical vine has giant trumpet-shaped flowers that hummingbirds and butterflies adore. The vine itself and leaves are a little sparse, though — not a great vine for privacy.

Morning glory. You can't plant just one. They form a tangled mess and will be covered in flowers that, as their name implies, bloom in the morning (later on a cloudy day). Careful, though: Each flower will drop a seed that rolls into some crazy spot and next year you'll have morning glories everywhere.

Passionflower. This has one trippy-looking flower. The vine grows quickly and provides great cover as well as, well, passionfruits.

For people trying to achieve a quick cover on something, a **perennial vine** is a sure thing, together with an **annual vine** for the quick fix. This combo always works.

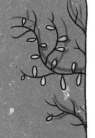

Clematis = *Clematis* species. Honeysuckle = *Lonicera heckrotti* or *sempervirens*. Hops = *Humulus lupulus*. Wisteria = *Wisteria* species. Boston ivy = *Parthenocissus tricuspidata*. Virginia creeper = *Parthenocissus quinquefolia*. English ivy = *Hedera helix*. Hyacinth bean = *Lablab purpureus*. Mandevilla = *Mandevilla* species. Morning glory = *Ipomoea tricolor*. Passionflower = *Passiflora* species

For more on privacy, try What Neighbors? (page 114).

  **grow what?**

Let this boggle your mind!
You can grow:

Apples
A lot of work, but they sure are tasty

Asparagus
Plant it once, and it'll come back better every year

Basil
Fresh is best

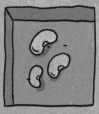

Beans
The magical fruit

Carrots
Eat your carrots: they're good for your eyes

Chives
Plant them once, then learn to love them in everything you cook; tough as nails

Corn
Don't take it on unless you're Jedi level or have an acre to devote to it

Garlic
Keeps vampires out of the garden, so a must-have, right?

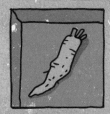

Horseradish
It's perennial and a bully; plant it once and look out . . .

Lemons
Sure! Even in a cold climate, with a little extra work

Lettuces
Be a salad-making machine

Melons
Watermelon, honeydew, cantaloupe, musk, Persian . . .

Mushrooms
Okay, not technically plants, but you can still grow them

Okra
Gumbo maniacs, unite

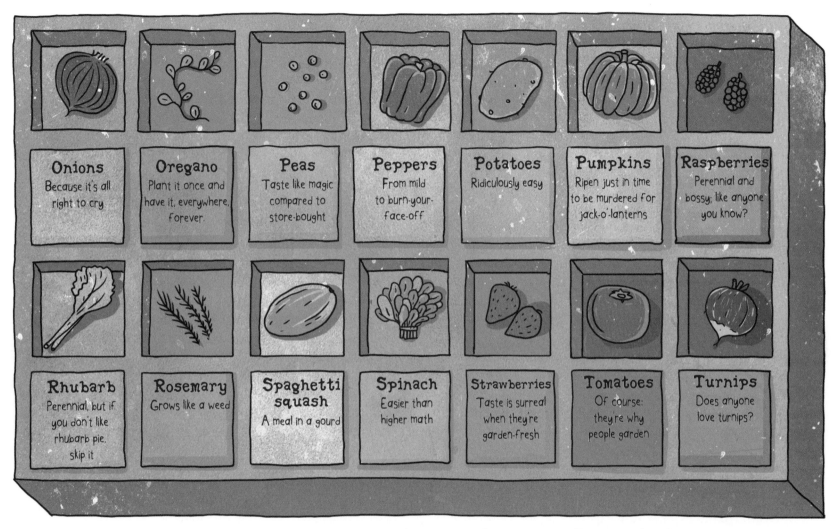

Onions
Because it's all right to cry

Oregano
Plant it once and have it, everywhere, forever.

Peas
Taste like magic compared to store-bought

Peppers
From mild to burn-your-face-off

Potatoes
Ridiculously easy

Pumpkins
Ripen just in time to be murdered for jack-o-lanterns

Raspberries
Perennial and bossy; like anyone you know?

Rhubarb
Perennial, but if you don't like rhubarb pie, skip it

Rosemary
Grows like a weed

Spaghetti squash
A meal in a gourd

Spinach
Easier than higher math

Strawberries
Taste is surreal when they're garden-fresh

Tomatoes
Of course: they're why people garden

Turnips
Does anyone love turnips?

Heirloom varieties are oldies but goodies, having proved over generations to kick butt. Seeds are saved from year to year, and they're cool. They provide genetic diversity, meaning that if everyone planted the same kind of seed (of, say, peas) and some disease knocked out all the crops, there'd still be other varieties of peas to take over.

Of course there's way more. Really, you could grow kiwis and kumquats . . .

Oh boy. I bet that's going to taste dee-licious! But before you feed yourself, learn about feeding your new garden at Fertilize It (page 148).

Or turn to Weeds Happen (page 154) to be prepared for what you may bump into.

Definitely check out Less Irrigation through Irritation (page 134) to make sure you don't kill your hard work.

herbie, fully loaded

Growing fresh herbs — like growing your own tomatoes — is one of the things that draw people into gardening. Some herbs need different site conditions from what veggies require (many like it on the dry side), but they're not difficult to grow. Give 'em a whirl!

A = annual;   P = perennial

Basil (A)

Basil grows well in full sun and average moisture. It needs a large pot (like a small bucket) or a decent spot in the ground. Its only special care is to pinch off its buds or flowers. This keeps the plant in the business of producing tasty leaves instead of switching gears to seed production.

Chives (P)

This is a tough perennial that you can plant in any sunny situation (in the ground is best), then ignore. Snub it. Until you want to use it. Even the flowers are edible.

Coriander/cilantro (A)

Super twins! This is a love-it-or-leave-it herb. As a baby, it's cilantro. Use the leaves sort of how you'd use sprouts. Once the plant matures, it bolts (goes to seed) and the seeds are called coriander. Tasty! The leaves will become fine and ferny, not so easy to use. To keep a constant supply of cilantro, plant seeds every 2 weeks throughout the summer. And either use a large pot (a small one won't cut the mustard) or plant directly in the ground.

Dill (P)

Throw some dill seeds into a hole and you'll have tall, graceful plants for the rest of your life. It self-sows rampantly. To get rid of it, cut off the flowers before they drop their seeds. You really must plant this one in the ground.

Mint (P)

There are many, many "flavors" in the mint family, and they're all a beginner's dream herb. Stick mint in a pot that's at least 6 inches in diameter, put it in full or partial sun, and water well. Mint, here it comes. Want to plant it in the ground but keep it under control (its scented tentacles will strive for world domination)? Plant it in a pot first, then sink the pot into the ground. Maybe it'll keep within bounds. Maybe.

Want to grow herbs indoors? It's not *quite* as simple as you'd think. Pick a sunny, high-humidity spot (like near the kitchen sink). The herbs that like it on the hot and dry side (rosemary, sage, and thyme) rely on humidity, not water, to survive the winter. In other words, mist them frequently, water sparingly.

For an indoor pot, start with mint and work your way toward the more ambitious projects.

Oregano (P)

This is another herb that likes to live large. In the ground, in full sun, you'll have an oregano farm in no time. Try planting it in a pot before you sink it into the ground, and be sure to harvest often, so it doesn't get a chance to drop seeds here, there, and everywhere.

Parsley (A)

With flat leaves or curly, this super-tough plant requires average water and full sun, and grows great in a container. Plant extras: Butterfly larvae (caterpillars) love to munch on it.

Rosemary (P)

This plant likes a life similar to that of thyme (see below) — hot and dry. Snip it often to encourage a ton of new growth.

Sage (P)

Sage also likes hot and dry, so if you want to make a combo herb pot, you can't go wrong with sage, rosemary, and thyme. Stick the pot in a sunny spot and water when you stick your finger in the soil and feel very little moisture.

Tarragon (P)

Underused and underappreciated, tarragon is a rambunctious herb that needs to be harvested regularly to keep it from becoming too shrubby. For best results, plant it in the ground in full sun, and give it plenty of water.

Thyme (P)

Thyme likes it hot and dry. It does best in a well-drained soil and loves, loves, loves to grow among stepping-stones, as long as they're in full sun.

Desperately Seeking Shade

Is relief from the sun your landscaping objective? Sure makes you cranky to spend time outside when you feel as if you're in the middle of a solar flare. I've known people who built a gorgeous giant pool and then never swam in it because it was too hot out there. Too hot to go in the pool? Dang, that *is* hot.

What you need is a shade tree and, like, 50 years for it to grow. (Insert groan here.) Regardless, check out Big, Big Trees (page 80). In the meantime, consider a shade sail, which is a triangular piece of outdoor-tough fabric that you install over the patio.

If you decide to plant a shade tree for future owners of the house to enjoy, select a spot where the tree will shade the house, patio, or pool during the hottest part of the day. Aim for the southwest or southeast of whatever you want to shade. While you're at it, think about shade for any hardscaping: An asphalt driveway, stepping-stones, walks, a concrete or slate patio, all heat up in summer until it feels as if you're walking (or sitting) inside a pizza oven. Planting shorties like small trees (page 98), shrubs (page 79), perennials (page 119), and ground covers (page 132) also help shade hardscapes around the house, helping you to be more energy efficient (they can cut down on air conditioning) and to *have* more energy.

The west-facing wall of my house is covered with a dense planting of Virginia creeper. In summer, I swear it makes the house a billion degrees cooler.

nine ways to get some shade

1.
Shade **sail**

2.
Pergola

3.
Plant tree and wait 50 years

4.
A giant inflatable Godzilla

5.
A planet-sized battle station moves in between you and the sun (That's no moon . . .)

6.
Live underground

7.
Grow vines on a trellis

8.
Make a giant tent out of bed sheets that envelopes the whole yard

9.
Don't go **outside**

Sure is cooler out here. Now you want to plant a shade garden? Saunter on over to Kinda Shady (page 92). *
For grass, turn to No Dearth of Turf (page 115) * Dry shade is not fun for plants, so visit Less Irritation through Irrigation (page 134). * Or if you want shade but copped out on doing the work, read Hire a Guy (page 22).

What Neighbors?

I live in a neighborhood where the houses are a little closer than I'd like them to be.

And as they say, good fences make good neighbors. I'm pleased to have a nice tall fence on one side — oddly, it's the side with the neighbors I like most. Coincidence? I think not! On the other side, the neighbors have tall arborvitae screening their view into my yard. Which is nice, because those dense evergreens sponge up some of the noise from their kids screaming 18 hours a day. Here are some ways you, too, can screen out the folks next door:

FENCING. You'd be amazed at how inexpensive a fence panel can be. It's the labor that's tough. Digging fence-post holes is one of the circles of hell. Then there are those not-so-pretty chain-link fences . . . See Vines, below, on how to disguise them.

GRASSES (ornamental). These make a terrific screen if they're tall enough. They soak up a ton of noise and provide a home for all sorts of wildlife. You've got to cut down those babies in March, though, so the new growth can come in. As a result, you may be feeling a bit exposed for a few months, right when you need the privacy.

TREES AND SHRUBS. Whether or not they're evergreen, they do a great job of screening the view. Just make sure they're low-branched enough to make a difference. I like arborvitae, hornbeam, clumping bamboo, hemlock, and viburnum.

VINES. A tall chain-link fence is great for keeping everything — dogs, babies, and shuttlecocks — in the yard, but it's see-through. Grow a ton of vines on it and everyone wins.

Ready to take this on? Read about the plants that will help you make your own slice of privacy. See Wee Trees (page 98), Lean, Mean & Evergreen (page 60), and Antisocial Climbers (page 106). Want privacy without the work? Run, don't walk, to Hire a Guy (page 22).

If you're running short on space, ask a neighbor if you can plant those screening trees on his side. Some (a few) people will say, "Sure, it'll up my property value."

No harm in asking, right?

NO DEARTH OF TURF

Sod or seed? Shade or sun? Here's what you need to know to grow a killer lawn: watering, fertilizing, and weed management.

It's just grass, but everyone freaks out over it. Let's start at the beginning — to seed or to sod?

Personally, I like sod. It's like getting a facelift in an afternoon. Drawbacks? It's more expensive than seed (still pretty cheap, though). It's a lot more work to lay, for sure. It requires almost constant watering at first, especially if the weather is warm. And there's little choice in the type of grass: You're usually stuck with whatever's at the nursery. On the other hand, you can lay it no matter the weather. I mean, don't put it on top of a snowdrift but . . . And if you have any slope going on, sod's the only way to go. Roll it out and stick some landscape staples in it (available at any hardware store: Ask for Landscaples).

Then there's seed. Seed is cheap. And you can choose whatever type of grass suits your fancy. On the downside, you're stuck with seeding in spring or fall; to get seed to germinate in the heat of summer is frustrating. As with sod, watering is crucial. And on a slope? Ha! Try getting seed to work. Every time you water or it rains, it'll slide down to the lowest point. The good news: The grass in that low point will be fabulous!

When you buy seed, look at all the different mixes. There's one for sun, one for partly sunny, and one for shade. Some have annual grasses mixed in for instant results. This annual grass shoots up overnight while the perennial grasses make themselves comfortable and stay for the duration.

Laying sod in late, late fall is for geniuses. It works like magic.

Turn to Prep School (page 126) to discover how to prep for seed or sod.

To learn about fertilizing that new lawn, flip to The Grass Is Always Greener (page 129).

ROCK ON!

Here's the thing about working with stone: IT IS SO DANG HEAVY!

The first step is to find a rock yard or landscape supply center. This is not one of those things you can tackle at the big-box store.

Promise you'll find a real rock yard. Or I'll totally unfriend you.

You've got to pick your project and pick your stone. Remember Game Time (page 18),

where we talked about complementing the architectural style of your house? This is a time when that comes into play. Your patio, walk, or wall should match the style of your house, like it was born that way. If your house is old and brick, you best be looking for old bricks. A flagstone chimney marries you to flagstone. A modern house is usually conducive to bluestone.

If you bring them the square footage of the project you'll be working on, the stone-yard peeps will help you figure how much you'll need and arrange delivery. Because there is NO WAY you can get stone home on your own.

Natural stone looks great with everything, although it's pricey. Man-made, or interlocking, pavers are uniform in appearance and therefore can't look natural. I think this makes them look sterile,

and dated, as dated as vinyl flooring. I frequently see a patio and ask, "Nineteen ninety-seven??" Vintage pavers, on the other hand, add character. These old bricks or cobbles are reclaimed from buildings, and have proved their staying power. You can often get them at a great price.

There's also stamped concrete, but don't let me catch you with this. It's just tacky.

Can't handle it (and that's not unreasonable)? Turn to Hire a Guy (page 22).

If you're full of can-do and want to design and plant some beds on the side of that new path or around the patio, see Design Hints (page 82). To add color, flip back to Sunny Day Real Estate (page 100).

When the project's done and planted, turn to Still Life with Mulch (page 125).

To be able to see your (or your hired guy's) handiwork at night, check out This Little Light of Mine (page 58).

STONE DOS & DON'TS

~DO~
get a loan from Grandpa Moneybags; this stuff is expensive

~DON'T~
use lava rock, unless you live on a volcano

~DO~
use locally sourced stone

~DO~
recycle old pavers

~DON'T~
use man-made stone

~DON'T~
underestimate how heavy stones can be

not your stepping stone

The easiest stone project is the basic stepping-stone path. All you need is stone, a shovel, sand, and a strong back. You can lay a stepping-stone path on soil, grass, gravel, mulch, moss, or ice cream. Lay out the stones in a pattern you like, then dig around them using the depth of the stone as your guide. Remove each as you then dig deep enough that you'll have room to put about 2 inches of sand at the bottom of the hole (this enables you to get the suckers flat). Put a stone into its hole and jump on it. Rinse, lather, repeat.

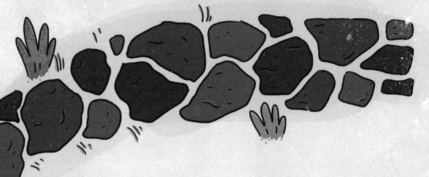

When you design a path on grass, set the stones low enough to be able to mow over them; otherwise, you'll nick the heck out of the lawn mower's blade.

You can use any flat stone for this project, in natural form or cut: flagstone, bluestone, bricks, man-made steppers, or fieldstone.

forever yours, perennials

Perennials are never gonna give you up, never gonna let you down, never gonna run around and desert you. They're here to stay — unless you kill them. Plant them once and they grow and grow, coming back every year. That low-maintenance aspect (except for weeding and occasionally dividing them) is what's different from annuals, which bloom, die, and must be replaced each year).

PROS

* Come back every year, are a one-time investment

* Get bigger and bushier over the years, most annuals are pretty small

* Multiply as they grow, so you can divide and move them to fill more space over time

* Some are evergreen or look nice in winter

* Some have colorful foliage and look great when they're not in bloom

CONS

* Usually have a short bloom season

* Are pricier to start with

* May need to be divided, which, with some plants, can be tedious

On the other hand, annuals bloom all summer long and perennials usually flower for a month or so and then sort of sit there.

Hey, that sorta sounds like my marriage.

Deadheading is removing a flower that's finished its business. When you remove flowers, you're redirecting a plant's energy to make more flowers. If you don't deadhead, the energy will go to making seeds.

Want to learn about sun perennials? Check out Sunny Day Real Estate (page 100). Shady perennials? Watch your wallet and turn to Kinda Shady (page 92).

Harder to do & LONGER lasting

A Path and a Patio are basically constructed in the same way, so here are the instructions for both. You dig out the desired area, going about 12 inches deep, then add 8 inches or so of crushed limestone. You'll have to rent a compactor to make sure the limestone stays put.

After it's packed in there, slowly add coarse sand and compact again. Then add an inch of sand. Once that's done, lay out the stone, adding or subtracting sand as you go to make the stones level. It's a big puzzle and it takes forever, but it's way cheaper than hiring a guy.

> Measure, level, measure, level.

After all the stone is in place, dump sand over the top of the new patio (or path) and sweep it into place. Go ahead and use regular play sand, or be crafty and find some polymeric sand. The polymeric stuff acts kind of like grout. Sweep into place and wet it down: It does a great job of staying put — and it helps prevent weeds.

To keep your work level, create a complicated-looking guide using stakes and string. Put in the stakes and then tie strings to them, making sure the strings are at the same height throughout. And by "making sure" I mean *measure*, don't just eyeball the situation. Then hold a level to the strings to make

sure everything is flatter than a pancake. Where do you tie the string? At the height you want the walk or patio to be PLUS an inch. (That extra inch is for work space, so that you can easily slip your hands [and a giant piece of stone] under the strings and be guided by them.) If you're the least bit off, you'll make a hash of it.

Have I lost you? No need for flop sweat. Hustle on over to Hire a Guy (page 22).

CAN YOU HEAR THE SUSTAINABILITY?

Hey man, you can use this water for your garden.

Rain barrels are sustainable, too. And they're fun. I'm all for barrels, no matter what's inside.

Let's talk briefly about something that, frankly, sounds boring. That something is sustainability. I'll try to make it as exciting as possible.

Sustainability is doing things in a way that makes the most sense for both you and a tree-hugging hippie. For example, use native plants because you know they'll take to your soil without extra work on your part. Use locally sourced stone instead of the stuff that's trucked in from far away.

Using trees to lower your cooling bills isn't you being cheap; it's you acting in a sustainable manner. Using solar lighting in the landscape is totally sustainable. So is avoiding pesticides. So are reusing, repurposing, and recycling. Want me to stop now? You get it, right?

Composting is über-sustainable and I'm suggesting, prodding, urging you to learn how to do it. If you skipped it, read Compostest Is the Mostest (page 70) now. NOW.

Still don't get it? Take the Sustainability Quiz on page 123.

~Sustainability Quiz~

Which is sustainable? Circle your answer(s).

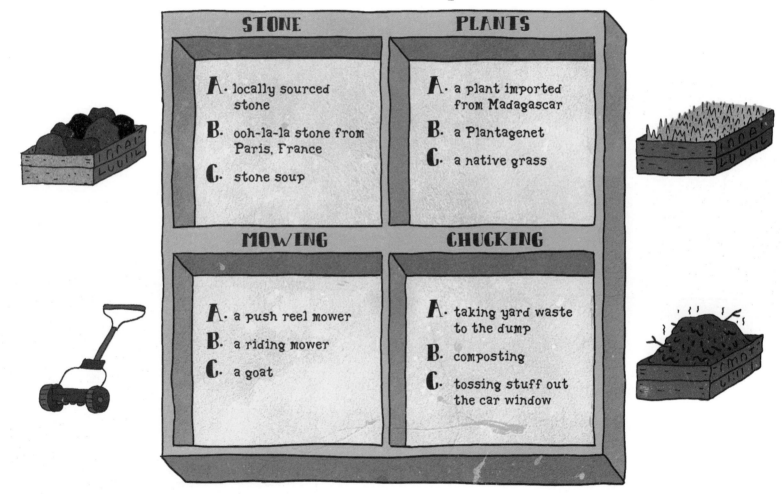

STONE

A. locally sourced stone

B. ooh-la-la stone from Paris, France

C. stone soup

PLANTS

A. a plant imported from Madagascar

B. a Plantagenet

C. a native grass

MOWING

A. a push reel mower

B. a riding mower

C. a goat

CHUCKING

A. taking yard waste to the dump

B. composting

C. tossing stuff out the car window

BOLDER BOULDERS

I see a lot of new houses with weirdly placed boulders. Now, I'm no landscaper ~ wait, what? Okay, actually, I *am* a landscaper. But I digress...

Rocks need friends, too! Don't just plunk them in the yard and walk away ~ tuck some plants around them, so they feel more at home.

If you live in a desert or on a mountain, rock it up. If you live someplace flatter than a cheesecake, think twice about how a rock group would look in your yard. Some houses with boulders in the yard look like they're at a costume party and wish they were anyplace else.

What are people trying to say with these boulders? For centuries, people have recovered stones from their fields and yards and tried to get rid of them. Now we have a people willing to pay beaucoup to have them put back in.

That's better. If you're going to have boulders in your landscape, be artful about it.

Still Life With Mulch

Here's the 411 on mulch and mulching - what to use, when to use it, and how (and how not to).

Mulch is a layer of something you put down so

A. you don't have to look at bare soil

B. roots have protection from too much heat

C. water doesn't evaporate too quickly

D. weeds are suppressed

Mulch emulates that cover of leaves and gunk you find on the forest floor. So, you want mulch, fer sure. But what kind? I like aged compost, but chipped pine-bark mulch is nice, too. I really prefer the finer-textured mulches; they look tidy and will mix into the soil if you want to move a plant. The mulch you see more often is shredded bark. It has a coarser texture and the color often fades as the sun bleaches it out. You can also use stone to mulch; you'll never have to reapply it. But you'll also never be able to get rid of it. You can't just throw away 2 yards of gravel.

They make rubber mulch now, and that's fine (I guess). But use it only in a playground situation. For more about it, see More Bounce for the Ounce (page 149). For more about it, see More Bounce for the Ounce (page 149).

I don't get the red-mulch thing. Why would you want a dyed product in your garden? I like my dyes in my food and in my hair, not in my garden.

How do you keep things looking good? Go to Living on the Edge (page 135). Mulch helps retain moisture. How are you watering? Hop, skip, or jump over to I Put My Root Down (page 127).

Prep School

Preparing an area for seeding or sodding is more important than I wish it was. I just want to lay sod on top of my existing sorry lawn. Sadly, that won't quite work. You've got to make sure there's something for those little roots to grab onto. Whether you seed or sod, the soil will probably benefit from a quick pass with a rototiller to loosen it up. For deluxe soil, spread composted manure on the surface, then till it in. Next, rake and rake and rake until it's as smooth as butter. If you find any lumps, bumps, or chunks, keep raking.

Sometimes shortcuts work, though. I recently prepped my sorry lawn for sod by mixing up several bags of cheap topsoil and manure and spreading it right on top of the grass. Didn't even need a rototiller.

Review what you know about soil and amendments at Soil, Yourself (page 62).

Rather go to a movie? Check out Hire a Guy (page 22).

I PUT MY ROOT DOWN

Okay, your plants aren't new anymore, so let's stop babying them. Even if you're a smotherer. Here's the deal: As much as plants need water, too much of a good thing will kill them. The last thing you want is an episode of *Garden CSI SVU*.

The best way to tell if your plants need a good drenching is to stick a finger in the soil. Dry? Then water! Feel moisture? Go inside and watch yourself some *Simpsons*. When you water, aim for the roots, not up in the air or all over the mulch. Soak the soil around a plant until water holds for a few seconds and then move on to the next one.

If this seems to contradict every sprinkler you've ever seen, you'll understand why I'm confused. Leaves don't absorb water; roots do. So instead of a sprinkler gadget, check out a soaker hose. Available at any garden center or the big box, lay it down at the base of as many plants as it will reach and turn it on for 10 minutes.

And look into getting a timer for your hose, too. Best $30 you'll ever spend.

Need a rain gauge?
Why not try a can with a measuring stick in it?

Let's check to see how wet the soil is. Stick a finger in it. If the soil is wet just on the top bit, you lose ~ water some more. If it's wet down to your fingertip, stop watering.

Want to learn about automatic watering? Turn to Timer after Timer, page 128. For info about drip irrigation, see Drip It Good (page 131).

looks like he was underwatered

Timer after timer

An irrigation timer is cool. Basically, this handy little device is an alarm clock that waters your plants. Screw it onto the spigot and then the hose in the back end, set it, and forget it.

All hardware stores sell them and they come in a ton of price points and capabilities — from the kind where you turn an egg timer to 20 minutes and the sprinkler then waters for 20 minutes, to a multihose octopus that waters different zones on alternate days for varying amounts of time.

The average timer is battery operated. You store it for winter, and in spring you install it between the hose and the faucet. Set the appropriate time (see Breaking the Mold, page 138) and plants will be watered consistently until you uninstall it in the fall. This is great for when you go on vacation.

Plants, like dogs, want to be watered on a consistent schedule. If you've ever had a dog, you've seen that it knows when it's feeding time. Delphiniums are considerably quieter about it.

Dizzying?

It's fine to pass on the chore of installation. See Waterworld (page 137).

Getting bored with all this? Why not make a chore cootie catcher (page 140)?

Keep in mind that a timer doesn't know that it's been raining daily for a month. Do monitor the situation.

the grass is always greener

Even if you don't have pets or kids, I hope you can see the benefits of an organic lawn. It's better for you, the Earth, and your wallet. All it takes is a topdressing of compost, a few times a year, to keep you looking green. Just shovel it onto the lawn and rake it until you see 97 percent grass and 3 percent compost, and you've won! Now water it in and you'll be amazed at how soon you'll see results.

If you're pounding the turf — playing badminton, wrestling, or holding garden parties all over the place — the lawn will need core aeration now and then. "Core aeration" is just a cool way of saying that you rent this machine and run it over the lawn, and as you do this it pulls out little plugs of lawn and soil that look remarkably like dog poop, and this greatly improves the whole world. Water will be able to penetrate the lawn better, give those roots some wiggle room, and relieve compaction.

Dog owners, people with kids, and partyers will get the most out of aeration. The more lawn traffic you have, the more you need it. Once in spring and once in fall and you should be golden. Everyone else: Aerate every few years.

Composted chicken poop makes a great lawn fertilizer. When you're applying it, though, wear your tall boots and a face mask. Dump a bag of it into a fertilizer dispenser (the kind you push) and go crazy. Haunt garage sales, where you could get one for $5. If that fails, hardware stores sell them for about $30.

When the aerator brings up the plugs, you're going to be tempted to rake them away. Don't — when they decompose, they're compost for the lawn.

Weed Worries

I don't know why people freak out about lawn weeds.

As long as they're green and all the same height, who cares? If they're getting on your nerves, though, here's the sane person's guide to getting rid of them.

Set the mower blade to its highest position. This will enable the grass to shade out any baby weeds. Don't let weeds flower and set seed. Even if all you do is rip off their heads and throw them away, you'll be helping.

Don't go crazy watering. Water deeply, but not often. You're watering weeds, too, you know?

You can't go wrong with digging them out. I pull them after we've had a few days of rain. They come right out.

Healthy soil supports the growth of a healthy lawn. Unhealthy soil creates a thin or patchy turf. On top of that, some weeds out there actually thrive in bad soil, and they're biding their time before they swoop in and take advantage of your lawn's pattern baldness.

There's a greener way, you know. Check out **LawnTurnatives**™ (page 132) for ideas on how to cover your space a little more ecologically.

Or flip to **Mow and Blow** (page 133) to learn how to maintain a lawn's green fabulousness.

Lawns need lots of water, so check out **Waterworld** (page 137)

Go get those new weeds over by the tulips

Are dog-pee spots on the lawn getting you down?
To prevent them, just do a little extra rinse after your dog pees. Or train her to pee on weeds. Then you're golden.

DRIP IT GOOD

So you're thinking about drip irrigation, eh? That's wise. You can do it yourself, inexpensively, and if you flub it, you can fix it for pennies. That's a ringing endorsement, right?

Drip irrigation involves a complicated series of hoses and tubes that lay on top of the ground (although you can camouflage them with mulch; see page 125). The setup will drip small amounts of water into the soil over a long period. This is super-efficient, because water is absorbed at the roots and doesn't end up all over the driveway and such.

First buy the little piece that attaches the drip hose to the faucet. Jam the hose end into it and you're off and running. You can purchase the tubing in giant rolls at any hardware store.

Next, cut and splice bits and pieces into the hose to customize the hose. Elbows, Ts, spaghetti tubing to reach baskets and containers, a soaker hose for around trees — the options are endless. All this rigmarole takes a crazy-face amount of time, but it's cheap enough that it makes up for it.

When you're in the hardware store, look for the parts and pieces for drip irrigation in the plumbing section, not the lawn-and-garden section. That took me about seven years to figure out. You're welcome.

There are great catalogs and sites devoted to drip irrigation. Some of them even have preassembled kits to get you started.

the DRIPS

Want to know about irrigation timers? See Page 128

To get the heck out of here, run to This Little Light of Mine (page 58).

LawnTurnatives™

Between you and me, lawns are *so* last semester.

All the cool kids are planting less-resource-intensive plants for less work and a greener planet. Mowing with a gas mower is baaaaaad. Watering during a drought is baaaaad. Instead, put in some ground covers or mass plantings of perennials.

Kill the existing lawn with an eco-friendly herbicide or cover the space with several layers of newspaper, held down by bricks or mulch. Occasionally peek underneath to check on how things are progressing (or not progressing).

Research which plants will do well in your area and will also complement the architecture of your house. Look into natives and other plants that don't require a lot of water. No sense in taking out the lawn and replacing it with something equally high-maintenance.

You may have to rototill between killing the lawn and planting.

Transform the front lawn into a cottage garden with annuals and perennials, a sea of perennial grasses, a native-wildflower sanctuary. Or fill it in with ground cover. You can even grow edibles.

If your yard is shady, you never had a shot with grass to begin with. Imagine a yard filled with ground-cover ivy and ferns with occasional boulders flanking a wandering path of mulch.

Eventually, this can turn out to be a huge money-saver. You'll save on mowing, watering, and, if you've been bad, lawn-care chemicals. I plan on buying a house just so I can rip out the front lawn.

Sometimes lawns just don't work. Hills, soggy spots, and dense shade are all ideal situations for LawnTurnatives. Better than pushing a square peg into a garden-shaped hole.

Did I not sell you? Then turn to The Grass Is Always Greener (page 129). To learn more about perennials, go to Forever Yours, Perennials (page 119)

Are you crunchy-granola and already green? You'll love Eat It (page 75).

Mow & Blow

Here's the minimum of weekly yard maintenance and how to accomplish it like a sane person.

   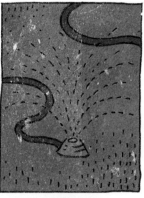 

STEP 1
Mow everything. Not too short. Use the highest setting. Get as close to the edges of the yard as you can, because Step 2 is a pain. As you mow, leave the clippings where they are; don't bag them. They'll decompose and return nutrients to the soil, which will feed the grass. It's the circle of life, yo.

STEP 2
Weed-whip everywhere you couldn't reach with the mower. I once weed-whipped my whole front yard because the lawn mower was accidentally under a pile of vintage dresses. That happens to everyone, right?

STEP 3
If you have an electric blower, use it. Start in one corner and blow all the debris toward the compost heap. Then scoop it up into the bin or pile. If you don't have an electric blower, clean up after yourself with a rake and a broom.

STEP 4
Apply any organic fertilizers you want to use and water them in. You probably won't do this every week; once a month during the growing season should be fine.

STEP 5
Margaritas!

> Actually, **STEP 1** should be, "Pick up any dog poop you may own, and any blade-destroying obstacles like toys, rocks, and random bits of rusty metal."

> A **short lawn** is nothing but trouble. It's actually healthier for you to leave it long. Taller blades of grass block the light from reaching weed seedlings so they don't get any ideas.

> It's cheap and easy to get someone to do the mowing. Interested? Flip back to Hire a Guy (page 22).
>
> If you're up to the challenge, make a Chore Cootie Catcher (page 140). Also check out Weed Worries (page 130).
>
> Tired of maintenance? Throw in the towel at LawnTurnatives™ (page 132).

Less irritation through irrigation

You planted it, now **keep it alive**. Okay, those plants you just put in? They've gone through a big transition. If it's summer and you did all this work? Holy freak-out. Your plants already hate you. Let's bribe them with some H_2O.

For annuals and perennials, be prepared to water every day, or at least to check on them. The soil around them should be moist but not waterlogged.

If you're watering a new tree, it's best to go slow and low. Once a week, set the hose to a dribble, put it about a foot from the base of the tree, and leave it on for a few hours, for its first summer. After that summer, you only really need to worry about it in a drought. If that's what you're contending with, water as you did when you first planted the tree. You don't want it to be stressed from thirst.

There are two kinds of people in the world: the misers and the smotherers.

A miser gets plants into the ground, and if they don't survive? That's their problem. Watering is an afterthought, not a priority.

A smotherer overwaters his plants. That's because it's the only way he can show love. Try words, yo.

Want some help, and maybe some automation? Turn to Waterworld, page 137. Or do you think you can do it yourself? Check out Drip It Good, page 131.

LIVING ON THE EDGE

Nothing can change the look of a garden as quickly as a good, clean edge.

The edge is where the bed meets the lawn. You can hand-edge it with an edging tool or a shovel. If you make that edge really deep and defined, it's called a trenched edge, and I'm a fan. Some people need a more defined edge and a rolled-rubber product. Yuck. Let's leave the rubber where it belongs, in your tires.

Some people like the look of bricks or pavers for edging. That's fine.

The important thing is to make sure pavers are set low enough (see page 120) that you can race over them with the mower and don't have to get out the weed whip. Keep in mind that pavers are expensive and unnecessary, and you won't find them in nature. Now that I think of it, you won't find an edged bed in nature, either. So let's move on . . .

You could have a bed full of weeds, but if it's freshly edged, it'll look intentional. It'll be all "I meant it to look this way. You like?" /// If you're not feeling up to it, get help at Hire a Guy (page 22). /// Mission accomplished? Move on to Still Life with Mulch (page 125). /// What's with your soil? Find out at Soil, Yourself (page 62).

CUT IT OUT

Pruning may sound like a daunting chore, but if you go slowly, it ain't no big thang.

Start with sharp, clean pruners and remove all the dead bits. If you're pruning branches from a tree — how can I put this? Well, let's just say your hand is a tree and your thumb is the branch to be removed. Cut as close to the tree as possible but at the narrowest point. Your goal is to have the smallest small area to heal. You also want the stub too short to hang your coat on. Just be sure you don't actually cut off your thumb.

Okay, that's deadwood. Next, cut out any branches that cross or rub against each other. After that's done, go ahead and prune anything that will improve the appearance. Snip off a single stray branch, get rid of any storm damage.

It's pretty important that you don't go at a tree or shrub with the intent to make it something it isn't — try to keep it in its natural shape and growth pattern. It's also important to not prune off too much at one time. Don't remove more than a third of the branches in one year; you'll stress out your poor woody friend.

Cuts should be at a 45ish-degree angle, so that when it rains, water runs off the cut and it doesn't get rotten up in there.

The best time to prune is late winter or early spring when you can see what's going on without all those pesky leaves in the way. The exception to this rule is for spring-blooming shrubs, like azalea, forsythia and lilacs. Prune them immediately after they're done flowering.

WATERWORLD

Is watering beyond you? It's fine to hire a service to come to your house, rip up the yard, and install an irrigation system. Or I guess you could let everything die. Up to you.

Do you have plants that constantly need watering because you're trying to achieve the impossible? A fern garden in the desert? Yeah, quit it. Cactuses are your friend, yo.

So the irrigation crew comes and they bring a machine called a trencher and they dig trenches all over your yard so they can install pipes everywhere you need water coverage. Depending on the size of your space, the irrigation dudes will probably break up the yard into "zones." This is so you can get great water pressure in each one.

There are several kinds of sprinkler heads. Pop-ups are at ground level until it's time for them to get down to business; rotor heads do the 360-degree thing; misters cover a small area. They all have a gazillion variables that one of the sprinkler dudes can tell you about. If you want to know.

Everything will be controlled by a timer box on the side of the house or in the garage. This is how the system knows when to go on (sunrise is best, for reasons I explain in Breaking the Mold, page 138), how long to stay on, and what days to go on.

Some are hooked up to a sensor so that it will know when it's been raining.

So, you'll need this crew to come back every spring to get you started and every fall to close you down for the year, so put that in *le budget*.

Break a head? You can get parts to fix it yourself at any hardware store. Or call the irrigation people for service.

If you didn't check it before, you need to read I Put My Root Down (page 127).

Want to know more about drip systems? See Drip It Good (page 131).

BREAKING THE MOLD

All kinds of plants get powdery mildew, which is a raging white fungus. The best way to prevent it is to space plants appropriately, as I've been harping at you to do since the beginning of this book. When plants have a good flow of air around them, humidity won't sit there causing problems.

If your plants are nicely spaced and still suffer from this mold, the culprit may be how you water. You want only the roots to get water, not the foliage. Check your irrigation system, should you have one. Is it activating at 10 at night? That's bad; if there's anything fungus likes, it's an all-night water rave at the base of your phlox. Set the timer for morning, so that any water on the foliage will evaporate quickly.

Lots of plants — phlox, peony, and squash, for example — get powdery mildew every summer as a matter of course. It might be ugly, but it won't kill them.

POWDERY MILDEW on a plant is comparable to athlete's foot on a person. It's ugly and uncomfortable, but the plant (and you) will survive. Let's review some simple sanitation practices. For the plant, throw mildewy leaves into the trash (not the compost heap). A fungus can spread from those leaves. As for you, stay out of the shower at the gym!

Going to the Dogs

Dogs and backyards go together like peanut butter and jelly. That combo wreaks havoc, though. If you want a designated place for your dog to exercise and poop, think about a fence. Check with your shire, city, town, or village to see what kind of fencing is allowed in the 'hood.

Some towns require a permit to put in a "permanent structure." Where no fences are allowed, or if you just don't want a solid barrier, you still could get a buried electric fence. Hire a company to put one in for you or buy a kit and do it yourself. It consists of a series of wires that you bury and a shock collar for the dog. When Fido sees his chance for freedom . . . BZZZZZZZ!

It's not the kindest thing you'd ever do for your dog, but it serves the purpose of keeping it off the streets (where more harm than a little BZZZT! can come to him) — and out of the vegetable garden.

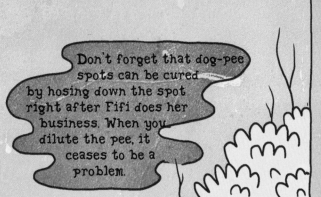

Don't forget that dog-pee spots can be cured by hosing down the spot right after Fifi does her business. When you dilute the pee, it ceases to be a problem.

Things to stay away from if you have a dog: **chocolate hull mulch**, **boxwood**, poisonous plants like **wisteria** or **yew**, **fertilizer** containing fish emulsion (you don't want to know what a dog that has been licking fish fertilizer smells like), **skunks**, and fencing made from **beef jerky**.

#

Okay, you've got the mowing and blowing down to a science and you're ready to take things to the next level. Frankly, there are lots of chores: pinching, deadheading, pruning, weeding, turning the compost, trimming the hedges . . . That's what life's like when you want an awesome outdoor space. Use this chore cootie-catcher to decide which task to tackle first.

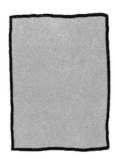

Take an 8 x 11-inch sheet of paper.

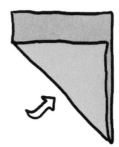

Fold corner up untill it meets the other side.

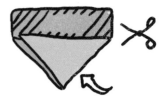

Fold other corner up so it meets the other side, then cut off the rectangle.

Unfold it.

Fold up all the corners so that the points meet in the middle.

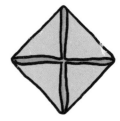

It should now look like this. Flip it over.

Fold up all the corners so that the points meet in the middle.

Flip it over. It should now look like this.

Now fold the top back.

Work your fingers into the corners from the folded side.

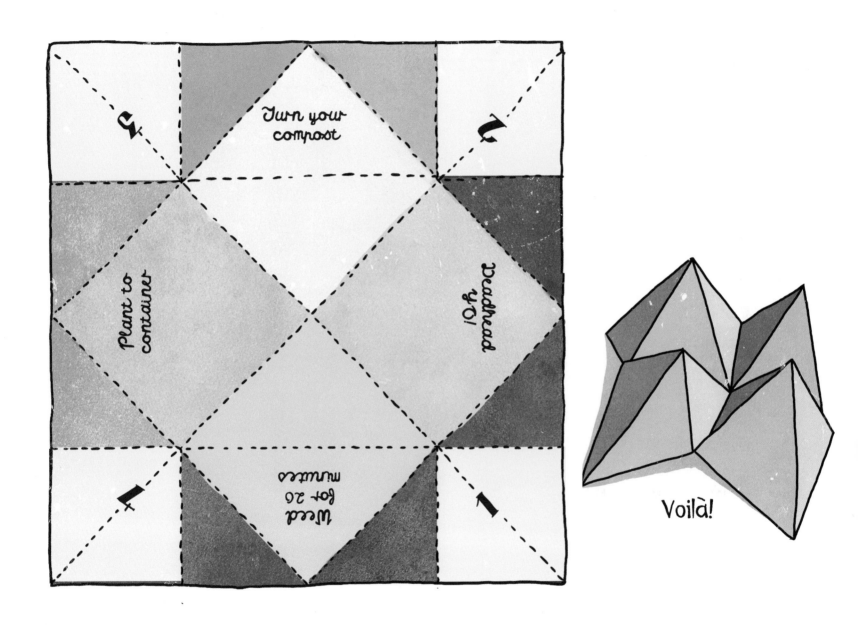

Turn your compost

Plant to container

Deadhead it!

Weed for 26 minutes

Voilà!

SMOKE & MIRRORS

Trying to sell your place in a hurry? Having the in-laws for a visit?? Hosting a summer party? Here are a few things you can do in a weekend to improve the view.

 1 Mulch it up (Page 125).

 2 Edge those beds (Page 135).

 3 Plant at least three containers (Page 49)

 4 Add lighting, even just cheap solar lights along pathways (Page 146)

 5 Add organic fertilizer to the lawn to make it green, although stinky (Page 148).

 6 Go on a pruning spree (Page 136).

 7 A little weeding wouldn't kill you (Page 154).

 8 Deadhead (Page 143).

To get out of doing any of this, invite people over only when the weather is bad, then stay indoors. For more ideas, try Decks in the City (page 49).

I saw a deadhead sticker on a Cadillac

Deadheading is the practice of removing spent flowers to get more of them. It also comes in handy for lusty self-sowers you don't want self-sowing lustily.

Basically, you're snapping off the spent flowers. The trick is to do this with sharp pruners or a dedicated pair of scissors. Make sure you cut back to a place where the plant will still look attractive. Don't leave a stalk poking up to the sky. You may have to cut that stalk all the way to the ground, in some cases. Like when an iris or daylily is done blooming.

If you want to be all pro about it, you'll clean your pruners or scissors with a spritz of rubbing alcohol after you've deadheaded each plant. This prevents one plant from contaminating another with a virus or fungus.

Deadheading often does some double duty ~ plants get pinched back in the process.

Want to learn about pinching? Go to Pinch Me (page 145).

For full-on pruning advice, turn to Cut. It. Out. (page 136).

TOP LUSTY SELF-SOWERS

Columbine
(*Aquilegia* species)

Black-eyed Susan
(*Rudbeckia* species)

Sneezeweed
(*Helenium* species)

Northern sea oats (*Chasmanthium latifolium*)

Goldenrod
(*Solidago* species)

Butterfly weed
(*Asclepias tuberosa*)

WHAT BIG TEETH YOU HAVE

You could do everything right, from the planting to the watering, and still end up with our woodland friends using it as an all-you-can-eat salad bar. How do you keep deer, rabbits, moles, voles, chipmunks, squirrels, and the yeti from ruining your dreamscape?

There is something to be said about planting what they don't like. Some plants actually keep critters away — mints and members of the onion family, for example. But what if you don't know you have a critter problem until after you've planted a tasty smorgasbord of deer-attracting lettuces?

There are sprays and powders that help to keep away the wee beasties, such charming items as coyote urine, creepy garden gnomes, products that smell like rotten eggs, and blends of spices. Some of these work — until it rains and washes away the product.

I say, get a Doberman. Or a fence.

There are a number of plants that mammals (supposedly) don't like to eat; sometimes you can find a regional plant list at a garden center. However, I've found that if a critter is really hungry, it'll eat anything.

When I have a critter problem, I go to the grocery store and buy cayenne pepper in bulk. I then spread it on the ground and on foliage. Every month or so I replace it, it seems to do the trick.

Got a problem with bugs? Turn to All These Bugs (page 153).

PINCH ME

Plants that are getting leggy should be cut back before they flop. Those perennials that bloom late in the summer or in the fall are usually the ones that need pinching. I give the evil eye to anything that looks like it's going to topple, then I cut it back by half. I cut each stem artfully. That means cutting one higher, one lower . . . Don't just take the hedge clippers and give a plant a flat top.

There's another reason to pinch: to promote bushiness before bloom. On an annual, when you remove buds for a few weeks, the plant will put forth more stems and more foliage. When you stop pinching, it will rush to fulfill its raison d'être (that is, its only goal), which is to produce seed. And to do that, it goes bananas putting out flowers on all those extra stems. Nice!

Plants that love to be pinched:

Aster (*Aster* species)

Joe-pye weed (*Eupatorium* species)

Garden phlox (*Phlox paniculata*)

Tall sedums (like *Sedum* 'Autumn Joy')

As a general rule, I never pinch anything after 4th of July weekend, to give plants time to set buds for fall.

Pinching takes a quarter of the time that staking does. **Staking is for losers**.

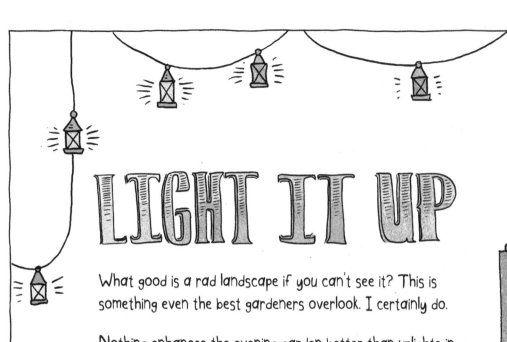

LIGHT IT UP

What good is a rad landscape if you can't see it? This is something even the best gardeners overlook. I certainly do.

Nothing enhances the evening garden better than uplights in tall trees, washes at walls, and matching rolls of path lights. If your nickname is "Sparky" and you know your way around a fuse box, well, then, go ahead and light it up.

The rest of us? We probably have to hire a guy (see page 22).

However, solar lights are available for anyone to install, and they're getting less lame every year. They'll never have the impact of real low-voltage lights, but they're a nice touch. You can flank a walk with them for a finished look.

Got a deck? Why not embrace the tackiness of summer? String patio lanterns on the rails, use tiki torches, put twinkle lights in the trees. Nothing wrong with getting a jump on winter decorating!

Aren't you proud? Make sure you're keeping up appearances at Mow and Blow (page 133). Don't want to light up? Go for more curb appeal with Smoke & Mirrors (page 142).

How about a water feature? Flip to Water, Water Everywhere (page 150).

Cleanup Time

People make a big show of the two annual cleanups, but it doesn't have to be a big deal.

In spring, spread a new batch of mulch, then go fly a kite. In fall? It depends on how you feel about leaves. I leave the bulk to lie around until spring because I'm lazy and because Mother Nature knows what's she's doing. Fallen leaves protect plants and when broken down are great for the soil. However, I have neatnik neighbors who think they must eradicate each and every leaf. With tweezers.

For fall cleanup, put any containers that are not winter hardy (like terra cotta and glazed pots) in the garage or basement for the winter, cut down the perennials that need it (very few), and throw dead vegetable plants on the compost heap.

Even if you hate leaves, don't bag them up like trash and send them off to a landfill. That's totally bogus. Either compost them or send them someplace to be composted.

Yearly cleanups are as much work as you want them to be. Usually people do them because their neighbors are doing them.

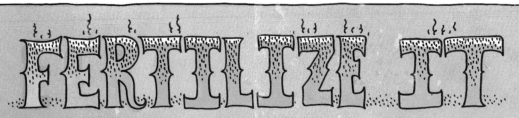

FERTILIZE IT

There are two kinds of fertilizer: organic and junk.

I hope it's clear that you want an organic fertilizer. They come from natural things, not chemicals.

You're looking for something made from compost, manure, seaweed, fish bits, or worm castings. You can get bags, boxes, and bottles of an organic fertilizer.

What's so great about organic fertilizers? Well, who wants chemicals to make their garden grow? To me, it's like giving steroids to a baby or Red Bull to a puppy. Organic fertilizers work well and you don't run the risk of chemically burning your plants. The nutrients in an organic fertilizer release slowly and naturally.

Bonemeal and blood meal are fertilizers, too. Bonemeal, a source of phosphorus, takes years to a break down, so don't expect instant results. Even though blood meal is a great source of nitrogen for plants, it's just too gross for me. It looks like a box of scabs. I guess I prefer to garden vegetarian.

Be on the alert for "greenwashing" — that's the crafty packaging and labeling of nonorganic products to look organic and good for you. For example, sewage sludge packaged as a "natural" fertilizer and a synthetic chemical labeled NATURAL HERBICIDE — that's greenwashing.

Stop squirming. It's not that bad.

Now read Weeds Happen (page 154).

MORE BOUNCE FOR THE OUNCE

Your kid wants a swing set, trampoline, or bouncy castle. Well, those things are the natural enemies of a green, lush lawn. Rubber mulch is the shiznit for this sort of situation; it's sustainable (see page xx), safe for kids to fall on, fun to look at. It's not my favorite for mulching plants, as I think using natural materials is the way to grow in the garden, but this is a reasonable application for it.

So, for a play area, determine how much you want to convert into a rubber mulch pit. Maybe try ye olde trick of laying a rubber hose in the lawn to figure out the shape and size of the eyesore. Next, dig down a few inches and remove the soil. Six inches is best, but I bet you'll give up at around three. The deeper you dig, the better the bounce your kid will get when he does a swan dive to nowhere and the fewer weeds you'll have to fight.

Some would argue that landscape/weed-barrier fabric should be used in this instance. In my experience, it's funky junk that keeps water from draining properly; you could end up with a giant mud pit with it. I'll take a few weeds over mud any day.

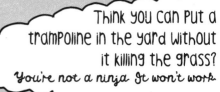

Think you can put a trampoline in the yard without it killing the grass? *You're not a ninja. It won't work.*

Water, WATER EVERYWHERE

The sound of trickling water (in the garden, not in the sink) goes a long way toward lowering blood pressure and camouflaging the noise from the freeway you live next to. There are several options for getting a little water running in the yard. Here are three:

Plug-in-and-go fountain.
Add water, plug it in, and feel the relaxation. Don't let it run with no water in it, though, or you'll need a new pump.

Small "pondless" water feature.
Dig a hole, drop in a rubber liner and rocks, and put in a pump, then the water recirculates in a waterfall or via a rock with a hole drilled in it. You hear the water but there's no pond. And that's great, because ponds are work.

Pond.
Ugh. What a lot of work. And because it's a ton of work, very few people do it right. You can make a pond with a preformed plastic insert for which you dig a hole that's just big enough. Or you can dig as big a hole as you want, put in a thick pond liner, and try to make it look natural with stones. This requires a major pump and filter, too, or else that stanky water will sit there and breed mosquitoes and, well, stink. And sure, you can have fish and cool aquatic plants, but you'll also have algae, birds that eat your prize koi, and winterizing. It's all work.

You must use actual pond liner, which is made of a thick rubber that comes in sheets. You can't use garbage bags, a tarp, construction plastic, aluminum foil, cling wrap, or pleather pants.

SPRAY + PRAY

Weeds happen! They just do. It's not because of something you did in a past life. It's best to handle things organically, the most organic method being to yank them out by hand. But there are also organic sprays like horticultural-grade vinegar and clove and orange oils. Keep in mind that these will kill anything they come in contact with — grasses, broadleaf plants, saplings. Some people use steam, flames, or hot water to kill weeds. I'm all for it. You can also smother them with cardboard or newspaper and top with a layer of mulch. To keep weed seeds from germinating, try sprinkling corn gluten in the spring.

I bet you've felt the temptation to buy a spray and kill, kill, kill the weeds. Well, you must know about chemical herbicides before you start nuking. My wonderful neighbor, Georgette, could tell you this story. There are two kinds of chemical herbicide: One kills only broadleaf plants, pretty much anything but grass. The other kind kills everything without a care in the world. Guess which one Georgette used on her lawn?

A year later, she's back on track.

Now, that being said, these herbicides have all sorts of toxic effects on wildlife. Also? Plants are becoming resistant to sprays. Yup, that's all we need: tougher weeds.

> When I was little, my mom told me to weed my sandbox before company came. I didn't. I procrastinated until right when the guests were expected. Mom told me to stand back, doused the sandbox with gasoline, and set it ablaze. Minutes later, I had a pristine sandbox.

The next page is about bad bugs, so don't read it right before bed.
Feeling like you want to wrap it up? Check out page 159.

APHIDS, SPIDER MITES, and SCALE

What I'm about to tell you will make you want to take a shower. So read it while you're less than clean. Wee bugs are living off your plants and pooping everywhere. Sometimes you think it's sap from the trees, but it isn't. It's called frass or honeydew and it's bug squirt. Now, that's not the part I'd be concerned with if I were you. But it's a tell-tale sign that something is very wrong. If there are shiny, sticky speckles of goo all over the place, you have problems:

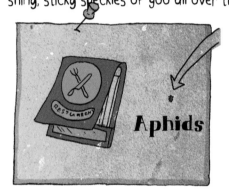

Aphids

Scale

Spider mites

These buggers come in more colors than Skittles, but they're much, much smaller. They suck the life out of your plants but are fairly simple to get rid of. If possible, spray a plant that's under attack with a strong burst of water and keep up with it until the aphids are all gone. You can also try insecticidal soap.

You can try an insecticidal soap to combat all these critters (as well as a few more). The fatty acids in the soap mess with the little guys. It's not toxic to us, though, or to our pets.

When it looks like your plants have little scabs all over them, they have scale. You'd never guess that these things are alive. And what's worse, their armor makes them impervious to almost everything. I have a solution, but it's disgusting. Rub them off, wearing cotton garden or latex gloves. Don't even look at the gloves when you're done. So gross. You have to keep at it with scale: Once it's there, you've got a battle ahead of you.

Mealybugs are scale that's white and fluffy. There are some on your ankle right now . . .

Man, these are a challenge to get rid of; if your plants are infested, consider moving. Or, if you're up for the battle, there are some natural enemies (insects you can buy on the Internet) that will help eradicate spider mites. There are also miticides, but you need to use them repeatedly for a long time. If your spider mites happen to be on indoor plants, you can use insecticidal soap or horticultural oil, repeatedly, but it's more likely that they'll just spread onto your healthy plants, and it'll be like a sci-fi movie up in there. Best to just chuck 'em and start fresh.

ALL THESE BUGS

You have to share the outdoors, but when bugs eat your plants, that's not cool, yo. Lots of bugs are harmless, even beneficial.* Here are some jerks:

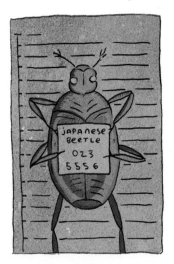

Insecticidal soap works on lots of nasty bugs, but in my experience, it's easier to pluck 'em and squash 'em.

Cabbage loopers/cabbageworms. Once I actually got angry at these caterpillars. I mean, I was yelling and stuff. Then I started squashing them with my fingers. That's hardcore. You can pick them up and stomp on them, too, or drown them.

Japanese beetles. These things don't stop. I collect them in a bucket of soapy water, then put their carcasses and some more soapy water into an old blender. Whiz it up, strain out the bodies, and use the black juice as a spray for roses. Ick. Disgusting, but it works. I guess the beetles smell their dead homies and stay away.

Slugs. You can pick them off and drown them, but they do most of their business after dark, so be ready to pull an all-nighter.

And here's an old idea that really works: Set a pie plate into the ground and pour beer into it. The slugs crawl down, get drunk, and then can't get out. What a way to go!

Tomato hornworms. Scariest. Caterpillars. Ever. They're huge and they hiss, but they turn into beautiful butterflies when they're done chomping on the tomatoes. They're best removed by purchasing them one-way tickets to wherever they want or by using your left boot on them.

* Beneficial insects include ladybugs, praying mantises, and green lace-wings. They eat the bad guys and do other gross things in the name of love. Like the wasp that lays her eggs in the eggs of a host pest and then her "kids" eat their "mamma" when they hatch.

WEEDS HAPPEN

Here are some common weeds:

Bindweed

I'm an organic girl, but bindweed makes me want to get out the gasoline and matches. This is the worst weed in the world. It climbs on everything and drops seed everywhere. If you try to pull out, it will come back stronger and then laugh at you. Even with my aversion to herbicides, repeated applications of chemical warfare are warranted here.

Bittersweet

This is a perennial vine that scrambles all over the place. It smells bad and it's sort of toxic, so don't go licking it. It's easy to pull out, though.

Chickweed

Gack. Chickweed is a major pain in the, um, grass because it starts early in spring, before you're even awake. It blooms early, too, so be vigilant and pull before flowering; each plant produces hundreds of seeds.

Clover

Clover is lying in wait until you let down your guard. It loves phosphorus, so make sure any fertilizer you apply is low in that element. It's almost impossible to get it out to the roots, so this weed is begging to be sprayed with organic herbicide.

I sort of like weeds, actually. They're the anarchy in a sea of perfection. They can take over, though (as anarchists do). Know your weeds, then figure out tactics for dealing with them. For weeds in beds, I strongly recommend getting addicted to hand pulling. It's amazing what you can do in 10 minutes.

Plantain

I shake my fist at plantain. This large-leaved plant is a perennial, so you can mow the flowers all day long and next year you'll still have a plantain. There's nothing to do but dig out this jerk. And all of its brothers and sisters.

Poison Ivy

This woody vine scrambles over trees, wooded areas, and fields. "Leaves of three, let it be," as in: don't even try to pull it because you'll be spreading its toxins everywhere. If you have poison ivy, call an Extension Service office and ask for advice.

Purslane

This succulent weed looks a lot like portulaca (moss rose). It thrives in hot and miserable spots. It has a long taproot, so it's wicked tough to yank out. To add insult to injury, if you break off any part of it, that piece can — and will — grow into a whole plant.

continue reading

WEEDS HAPPEN 2

Crabgrass
This thickly matting grass drives many home owners cray-cray. Regular mowing will keep it from flowering and dropping seed, and that's the end of the problem (eventually). You can hand-pull plants after a good rain; the rain loosens the soil enough that crabgrass comes right up.

Creeping Charlie
So, get this. This little puppy makes a poison to kill off plants around it to make room for itself. And that's why it's an awful turf weed. Pull him early and often.

Dandelion
This plant with the jaunty yellow heads that drive a lawn owner nuts came over with the early settlers to be used as a salad green. (And supposedly it's delicious, and packed with vitamins.) That taproot is impossible to pull out. You may think you've got it, but you'll leave a chunk, just enough for it to come back. Those fluffy seed heads kids like to blow on spread seeds all over the neighborhood, and maybe beyond. I wouldn't be surprised if they find dandelions on the moon.

Lamb's-quarter
This distinctive, silver-leaved plant is a piece of cake to yank before it gives you any grief. That grief comes in the form of a gigantic seed head that holds a mazillion seeds.

It's tempting to buy a giant jug of herbicide and just nuke the suckers, but take a step back and look at the bigger picture. That herbicide will rinse off in a rainstorm and then where does it go? Into our water system ... and then what? I think it's freaky, so I don't do it. Get 'em before they flower. No flowers, no seeds. No seeds, fewer weeds. Another thing that works well is a scuffle hoe: less bending when you hoe out those pesky weeds.

Ragweed
This is what makes you sneeze. Like you care, but most people think goldenrod is the problem. That's not you, though, right? This plant starts out lacy, recognizable, and easy to pull. Get it when it's a youngster; it becomes a beeotch.

Shepherd's Purse
I don't let this one bloom, and that seems to work. No flowers, no seeds.

Yellow Nutsedge
This perennial weed really gets my goat. Hey, wait. If I got a goat, would it eat all my nutsedge? Hmm. This grass grows quickly and will be taller than your turfgrass in no time. I've had great results, not to mention an aching back, from hand-pulling it.

AMANDA'S PARTY(ING) WORDS

Always:

1. Do what you want to do, not what everyone else does.

2. **Consider** your family, lifestyle, and pets when you're making yard-related decisions.

3. **Dream big**, baby!

4. **Compost**, if you can.

5. Wear **sunscreen**.

Never:

1. Plant more than two **topiaries** per yard, please. More than that is just crazy to look at. Same goes for weeping trees.

2. Use **red mulch**. Remember that red stinky sawdust they'd put down when a kid puked in grade school? Yeah, it's sort of like that.

3. Put in a **tree** without doing your homework. You may find yourself living in a treehouse one morning.

4. **Buy** mulch from a gas station.

5. Alternate purple barberry and yellow spirea, as a **special favor to me**.